Evil

Concepts in the Study of Religion

Critical Primers

Series Editor:
K. Merinda Simmons, University of Alabama

Books in the series Concepts in the Study of Religion: Critical Primers offer brief introductions to an array of concepts—modes of analysis, tools, as well as analytic terms themselves—within the discourse of religious studies. Useful for almost any course, the volumes in the series do not attempt to assert normative understandings but rather they introduce and survey the various modes and contexts for scholarly engagement with the concept at hand. How, for example, has the term "myth" been used, and what can various definitions allow us to do as scholars? Who in the field is working on the category of race and how? What might be the future of scholarship on gender in religious studies? What are the possibilities and limitations of description or comparison as methodological approaches? Thus, these critical primers provide—but are not limited to—concise overviews of the history of an approach or term. They also present the authors' own critical analyses of the dynamics and stakes present in discourses surrounding these concepts. Including lists of further readings to guide additional consideration of their topic, the books in this series are valuable resources for students and advanced scholars alike.

The series is published in association with the North American Society for the Study of Religion (NAASR).

Published

Comparison
Aaron W. Hughes

Interpretation
Nathan Eric Dickman

Evil

A Critical Primer

Kenneth G. MacKendrick

SHEFFIELD UK BRISTOL CT

Published by Equinox Publishing Ltd.

UK: Office 415, The Workstation, 15 Paternoster Row, Sheffield, South Yorkshire S1 2BX

USA: ISD, 70 Enterprise Drive, Bristol, CT 06010

www.equinoxpub.com

First published 2023

British Library Cataloguing-in-Publication Data
A catalogue record for this book is available from the British Library.

Library of Congress Cataloging-in-Publication Data

Names: MacKendrick, Kenneth G., author.
Title: Evil : a critical primer / Kenneth G. MacKendrick.
Description: Sheffield, South Yorkshire ; Bristol, CT : Equinox Publishing Ltd, 2023. | Series: Concepts in the study of religion | Includes bibliographical references and index. | Summary: "Evil: A Critical Primer argues that our colloquial conception of evil, as related exclusively to the moral domain, is usefully illuminated by attending to historical and cultural context and cross-cultural comparison"—Provided by publisher.
Identifiers: LCCN 2023009539 (print) | LCCN 2023009540 (ebook) | ISBN 9781781796184 (hardback) | ISBN 9781781796191 (paperback) | ISBN 9781781796207 (pdf) | ISBN 9781800504035 (epub)
Subjects: LCSH: Good and evil
Classification: LCC BJ1401 .M235 2023 (print) | LCC BJ1401 (ebook) | DDC 170—dc23/eng/20230725
LC record available at https://lccn.loc.gov/2023009539
LC ebook record available at https://lccn.loc.gov/2023009540

ISBN–13   978 1 78179 618 4   (hardback)
           978 1 78179 619 1   (paperback)
           978 1 78179 620 7   (ePDF)
           978 1 80050 403 5   (ePub)

Typeset by JS Typesetting Ltd, Porthcawl, Mid Glamorgan

Contents

Acknowledgements

Thanking those who have helped me along the way should be the easiest section of this book to write. It isn't. I don't mind thanking people, but the debt that I owe to those who have created the time and space for me to write is immeasurable and immeasurable is difficult to put into words.

I can start by saying that I didn't write this book alone. The text of this manuscript was read from beginning to end by half a dozen friends and colleagues (thank you Andrea, Hilda, Jason, Kathy, Merinda, and the anonymous reviewers). Material from this volume has been presented to thousands of students who have offered comments, written essays, and presented critical analyses of the required readings for "Evil in World Religions" since 2002. In addition to my undergraduate students, a host of teaching assistants, writing tutors, and research assistants have contributed to the contouring of each chapter. As well, friends, family, and colleagues—near and far—have offered time and energy to answer questions, provide references, and offer guidance or support along the way.

Of my graduate students, Jason Redden, Matt Sheedy, Ted Malcolmson, and Haley Driedger have been generous with their thoughts about purity and danger and patiently put up with a few detours into my work when asking for feedback on their own. Thank you. Thanks to my colleagues (past and present) in the Department of Religion: Brenda, Danielle, Dave, Dawne, Heidi, Ian, Jade, Johannes, Justin, Lisa, and Nicole. The short list of family, friends, and colleagues to thank includes Chris Brittain, Darlene Juschka, Bill Arnal, Randi Warne, Nicole Goulet, Steve Lecce, Skye Carrette, Jenny Baspaly and Michael Baspaly, Paul Lawrence, Alicia Brown, Andrew MacKendrick, and Cathy MacKendrick (hi Mom!).

I would also like to recognize family members who died before this book made it into print: Andrea's mom, Patricia; my sister-in-law, Danielle; and my dad, Louis (Kim). My dad didn't much care for vampires, he was more of a ghosts and goblins guy, but I think he would have found the chapter on disgust amusing.

Most of the writing for this volume took place during a six-month Research Leave in 2021. Additional scaffolding for "Evil in World Religions" was provided by a Scholarship of Teaching and Learning grant (2022), Teaching and Learning Enhancement Fund (2016), Teaching and Learning Innovation Project (2014), the Faculty of Arts Dean's Fund (2013, 2018), with additional supports from the Department of Religion and the Academic Learning Centre. When Kathy Block arrived in my class to talk about writing tutors, neither of us could have imagined the facilitated writing groups, targeted learning sessions, and peer review workshops that would follow. Working through this material with students and writing tutors has been a gift. A special thanks to Kathy and the writing tutors who have contributed to our writing experiments along the way.

In 2019 I attended an inaugural Indigenizing Curriculum Summer Institute. Organized by Cary Miller, Head of Native (now Indigenous) Studies, the ceremonies, readings, stories, and presentations brought into focus a reality I had chosen not to see. While I was aware of the genocidal effects of settler colonialism in North America, I was largely unaware of the particulars. As should be evident from what follows, I am indebted to this initiative, rooted in the Truth and Reconciliation Commission of Canada's "Calls for Action," for underscoring the significance of seeing things differently. What may be difficult to see from one angle can be painfully obvious from another. My experiences with the Institute encouraged me to rethink the aims of this volume and have obligated me to think critically about things I had taken for granted. Thank you.

Merinda Simmons, the most dangerous editor in the galaxy. You've made this soooo much better. Thank you.

The manuscript was drafted while binge-watching 12 seasons of *RuPaul's Drag Race*. Earworm: "Don't fuck it up." The editing process took place while binge watching several seasons of *My Kitchen Rules* (Australia). Earworm: "Where is the sauce?"

* * *

I'm tempted to list Andrea Brown as a coauthor. We've been collaborators in all things for over thirty years and there's almost nothing in this volume we haven't talked about. She's heard all the stories and helped me work through all the parts I've struggled with. Thankfully, my partner is no echo chamber. Upon examining an early draft of the Preface and Introduction she remarked that it was almost unreadable (this was correct). In every chapter she asked, "How is this going to dismantle misogyny?" When I lost the narrative, Andrea knew what questions to ask to get me back where I needed to be. It's been a privilege and a delight. She also held the cares of the world together while I was writing this book. Thanks Andrea.

Did I mention, she also laughs at my jokes? She's a keeper.

Nyx and Greta, thank you for all the artwork, books, candy, comics, D&D, funny animal clips, games, glue, hiking, LARPing, Lego, memes, music, paint, pasta, potatoes, puzzles, Star Wars, stickers, and swimming pools. I won't forget—something savory, something sweet.

A few years ago, our family purchased a bird feeder. It seemed like a nice way to bring a few of our flying friends into the yard. We didn't really know what we were in for. It didn't take long for the birds to show up and along with them came squirrels, rabbits, mice, deer, a fox or two, and a raccoon. We watched blue jays drop peanuts for the red squirrels, saw how a hawk will wait patiently before tearing off into the bushes to catch a sparrow, and noticed that bird droppings add a bit of seed variety to the ground beneath the feeder. These creatures all live in the neighborhood and at one time or another we'd seen most of them before, but the feeder became a focusing lens. We're learning about birds but also about how the creatures in the neighborhood are connected by land, water, flowers, and food. Watching the birds come and go has been inspiring in its own way. Like the feeder in our yard, this primer is designed as a focusing lens, drawing attention to the things that are already there.

Preface

The past few decades have given rise to hundreds of books about evil. Most of these books are written by moral philosophers coming to terms with the catastrophic events of the past few centuries. In these books we encounter essays on colonialism, genocide, racism, misogyny, and ecocide. And although evil can be used playfully to describe everything from the saturated fats in donuts to insipid popular music, it is often reserved for occasions when our moral and legal vocabularies fail us. Evil gives us a word for describing the indescribable. It gives expression to our innermost feelings. When evil is talked about in this way, it is our response to evil that constitutes the starting point of reasonable moral inquiry. So we are told.

Moral and political philosophers who write about evil in this way tend to fall into a trap familiar to scholars of religion. Throughout the history of the study of religion it has been commonplace to assume that religion is extraordinary, requiring an extraordinary set of tools to understand it (if it can be understood at all). This approach to the study of religion, known as the phenomenology of religion, stands in awe of what it purports to study. Religion is sacred. Religion is transcendent. Religion is so real there can be no theory of religion, not really. Religion is alive and if we accept religion for what it is, it will transform us. This legacy within the study of religion has been severely criticized because it removes religion from history and obscures the political interests underlying such a removal.[1]

The trap, when it comes to the study of evil, is the way in which the phenomenal reality of evil is assumed rather than set up as part

---

1. Russell T. McCutcheon, *Manufacturing Religion* (Oxford: Oxford University Press, 2003). For a critique in relation to comparison and the study of religion, see Aaron W. Hughes, *Comparison: A Critical Primer* (Sheffield: Equinox, 2017).

of a scholarly study. For example, in the introductory remarks to *The Anthropology of Evil*, David Parkin writes that, despite some societies not having a concept of evil, there is still an "irreducibility of the varying concepts of evil" that warrant comparative study. Similarly, Richard Bernstein writes, "There is ... something about evil that resists and defies any final comprehension."[2] Moral philosophers writing about evil often assume that evil exists without asking about how we come to recognize it as such. In this model, evil exists prior to our talking or theorizing about evil.

If we begin with the experience of evil as culturally invariant, the social history and politics of the category and the interests it serves fade from view. The naively placed spotlight focuses our attention on the dramatic spectacle, leaving the rest of the theatre in darkness. Even conscientious discussions of the "abuse of evil," highlighting how the term is used as a tool of unfettered manipulation, tend to underplay the subtle locations and indirect authorities that sanction discourses on evil.[3] This means that there are a lot of books on the topic of evil that don't really address the discourse on evil at all.

The critical discourse on evil I am contributing to does not refer to "actually existing evil"—as if realities exist apart from words—but to those who use the word to describe, explain, or condemn.[4] The discourse on evil refers to the record of the word "evil" in history. For example, throughout the late nineteenth and early twentieth centuries, Canadian school officials routinely described Indigenous culture as "evil." The concept became part of the justification for the implementation of a genocidal residential school system that persisted into the 1990s.[5] Few of the books written about evil address the convenience of having the word "evil" available for use in a taxonomy of hierarchies and rankings. It seems to me that the word is doing one of the

---

2. David Parkin, "Preface," *The Anthropology of Evil* (Oxford: Basil Blackwell, 1985), 1; Richard Bernstein, *Radical Evil* (Malden, MA: Blackwell, 2002), 7.

3. Richard Bernstein, *The Abuse of Evil* (Malden, MA: Polity Press, 2005).

4. A good introduction to this approach can be found in Russell T. McCutcheon, *Studying Religion: An Introduction*, 2nd edition (New York: Routledge, 2019).

5. Truth and Reconciliation Commission, *Canada's Residential Schools* (Montreal: McGill-Queen's University Press, 2015), 677, retrieved from http://caid.ca/TRCFinVol1Par12015.pdf.

things that it was designed to do: dehumanize others for political and economic gain. This dehumanizing quality does not exhaust its usage or the multiple frames of meaning assigned to the word; however, if we are going to continue to talk about evil, we need to recognize the wider scope of the term's context, politics, and utility.

As a starting point, we can say that discourses on evil belong to systems of intelligibility that categorize and rank states of affairs as much as they do people associated with the categories deployed. Simply put, a discourse is "a way of interpreting and ordering the world."[6] I assume that, embedded within these discourses, there are social interests and strategies of identification aimed at manipulating the fabric of shared social worlds: attractions, estrangements, challenges, and contradictions. In other words, there is nothing special about the discourse on evil, even if the concept has an esteemed place within the canons of moral philosophy and the philosophy of religion.

Furthermore, in European and North American contexts, the concept evil arrives with an unpaid debt to its theological legacy. Theodicy has been the regent discourse on evil for the better part of a millennium. Theodicy refers to a logical problem that attempts to reconcile three competing claims: God is good, God is all-powerful, evil exists. While moral philosophers recognize this history, rarely are the politics and prescriptions of its location worked through. The discourse on evil has a geographical and cultural location, and it plays a significant role in a vast array of social phenomena—from the politics of empire to the politics of gender. The politics of theodicy often define what gets to count as visible and invisible, relevant and irrelevant.[7]

---

6. Joseph Laycock, *Dangerous Games: What the Moral Panic over Role-Playing Games Says about Play, Religion, and Imagined Worlds* (Oakland, CA: University of California Press, 2015), 243.

7. The politics of theodicy as entwined with colonialism, misogyny, and racism is discussed in relation to the invisible world in Craig Koslofsky, "Offshoring the Invisible World? American Ghosts, Witches, and Demons in the Early Enlightenment," *Critical Research on Religion* 9, no. 2 (2021), 126–141.

In addition to the hierarchies presented in the discourse on evil and its theological lineage, evil has also been repurposed for the projects of modernity. In the modern context, moral and political philosophers work to translate the language of theodicy into the profane discourse of the public sphere. Once translated into a secular idiom, evil is then described in terms of will, conscience, and responsibility. The extensive narrowing of the term to apply exclusively to the individual is a uniquely modern twist to the concept.[8]

In the wake of the secularizing translations of Euro-Western modernists, contemporary moral philosophers often ask about the utility of the term and speculate about its explanatory and expressive power. These conversations about human rights, atrocity, and agency are often interesting and inspiring but can be unsatisfying. It appears that in the rush to create a viable taxonomy of evil or assess its ongoing relevance, the border authorities securing the category go ignored. Whatever the problem of evil, the *reality* of evil remains obvious to most people.

But why evil? Who authorizes this discourse? Where does its appeal come from? What maintains the discourse? In contrast to more conventional approaches to the topic of evil, this critical primer is designed as an introduction to a way of teaching and thinking about the subject differently. My aim is to reset the stage in preparation for a new story. To do that, we must turn on the house lights.

From the outset, I want to clarify what this book is *not*. It is neither a critical historiography nor a genealogy of the discourse on evil. I also do not directly engage debates within moral philosophy. Instead, I advocate a step back. The path taken here recalibrates the concept to see what happens. This critical primer is an experiment aiming to reintroduce evil by focusing on dangers and aversions. The emphasis here uses comparative analysis as developed in the study of religion to inform the discourse on evil. In so doing, it sets the stage for a revised account of the history of the discourse on evil, a history that would now have to include strategies of authorization and

---

8. For a study that questions the sufficiency of these kind of translations, see Talal Asad, *Secular Translations: Nation-State, Modern Self, and Calculative Reason* (New York: Columbia University Press, 2018).

classification.[9] This substantial reframing of evil is designed to bypass a narrow understanding of the term as circumscribed by moral and political philosophies that preserve theological assumptions in the discourse.[10] In reimagining evil through the concepts danger and aversion, I have structured this volume as a course of study designed to address this question: how is it that something comes to be perceived as dangerous or as something to be avoided? The rationale for focusing on dangers and aversions stems from a desire to include the widest possible array of human conceptions of health and harm within the horizon of an introductory study. In my view, notions of health and harm, captured in an emphasis on dangers and aversions, are the most compelling starting points for reintroducing and reconsidering evil.

In terms of the structure of this volume, I have used several key categories to organize the material presented. Each of these categories identifies patterns of interaction that create, maintain, or modify social norms and practices regarding dangers and aversions. The chapters discuss each in turn: classification and magical thinking, ritual, myth, strong emotions, and morality. After introducing and discussing a proposed key category, I then illustrate it with examples that highlight variety and variance in the ordering of dangers and aversions. On the whole, this critical primer is a bit like a field guide, created to assist in recognizing, describing, and redescribing what's out there in relation to something we're going to call evil. My aim is to introduce an orientation towards evil as dangers and aversions

---

9. In addition to the cited volume by Hughes, see Jonathan Z. Smith, *Drudgery Divine: On the Comparison of Early Christianities and the Religions of Late Antiquity* (Chicago, IL: University of Chicago Press, 1990); and Jonathan Z. Smith, *Relating Religion: Essays in the Study of Religion* (Chicago, IL: University of Chicago Press, 2004).

10. Nathan Loewen writes that in the last half century "the focus of the problem [of evil] is derived primarily by rendering a particular abstraction of Christian doctrine into the premise of theism." Then, when theism is removed (or translated) the explanatory system ceases to make sense. Nathan R. B. Loewen, *Beyond the Problem of Evil: Derrida and Anglophone Philosophy of Evil* (Lanham, MD: Lexington Books, 2018), 123.

that allows us to see things with an enlarged mentality (to borrow a phrase from Hannah Arendt).

This primer includes writings from several disciplines: Anthropology, History, Philosophy, Political Studies, Psychology, and Religion. Although I am uncomfortable with the rubric of world religions, the illustrations are drawn from case studies referencing Buddhism, Christianity, Hinduism, Islam, and Daoism. They are also drawn from a selection of urban and rural environments in Asia Minor, Europe, North America, and South Asia. About half of the illustrations have an explicit emphasis on gender. These choices are not intended to present an ideal paradigm of what gets included but reflect my own scholarly interests. Admittedly, but unavoidably, the gaps are almost infinite.

From the academic study of religion, the work of Bruce Lincoln and Jonathan Z. Smith has been especially instructive. I have used Bruce Lincoln's *Discourse and the Construction of Society* as a template for several aspects of this project, especially his focus on classification, myth, and ritual. To this I've added strong emotions as well as a section on morality, which may resonate with Lincoln's interest in cases dealing with marginalization, resistance, and authority. Lincoln's work illuminates the scope of strategies people use to organize and shape their social worlds. Jonathan Z. Smith's essay "The Devil in Mr. Jones" has also been a touchstone.[11] When confronted with inadequate explanations for the Jonestown deaths, including Billy Graham's suggestion that "Mr. Jones was *a slave of a diabolical supernatural power* from which he refused to be set free," Smith turns to comparison. The essay is an incredible example of the power of comparison to transform something deemed "utterly exotic" into something that is known and knowable.[12] It is my intention to subject the regent discourse on evil to a similar kind of transformation.

Keeping with Smith's interest in comparison, comparative analysis has four distinct movements: description, comparison, redescription, and rectification. Description has two aspects: (1) the circumscription

---

11. Jonathan Z. Smith, *Imagining Religion* (Chicago, IL: University of Chicago Press, 1982), 102–120.

12. Smith, *Imagining Religion*, 111–112.

of a particular example and (2) an account of the reception and interpretation of the example in question. In this volume I streamline this process by using a single account. The singular examples or case studies are then situated next to one another and redescribed using the key categories. The selected key categories have a long and complicated history in the study of religion and I am appropriating and repurposing them here in service of showing us something new about human worldmaking.[13] I also draw out similarities and differences within the key categories to showcase variety and engage in analytical work concerning, as David Frankfurter puts it, the "patterns that frame the differences."[14] I close each chapter by relating these redescriptions to dangers and aversions.

The process of comparison using key categories creates a map filled with examples that allow us to think and theorize about evil differently. It is a project that strives to find an adequate theoretical vocabulary to account for the massive variety in ascribed dangers and aversions across human cultures. Such a process is a more productive and critical way to engage discourses on evil.

By design, most of what follows does not participate in legacy debates about evil or moral philosophy. I am not bidding farewell to moral philosophy or theodicy, we're simply moving on to a new project. The closing chapter on morality takes a position within these debates, but I situate the discussion with the aims of this volume, treating morality as one key category alongside others. I therefore engage less with moral philosophy and instead offer more of an account of a particular kind of critical thinking that falls under the key category "morality." In other words, I cite morality here as a key category, not a master narrative framing my personal response to evil. Overall, I propose that, instead of assuming evil to be a real phenomenon and individuals to be free agents, we ought to instead look

---

13. As it is put by Aaron Hughes, "Comparison enables us to envision an issue or a problem (though, again, one largely of our own imagining) in our own dataset and reveals it as a larger issue relevant to human worldmaking." Hughes, *Comparison*, 54.

14. David Frankfurter, *Evil Incarnate: Rumors of Demonic Conspiracy and Satanic Abuse in History* (Princeton, NJ: Princeton University Press, 2006), 6.

at how we organize our relationships. What are we attracted to, and what do we avoid? What goes into our thinking about something as threatening? When we have a better understanding of dangers and aversions, we'll have a better starting point for studying evil within a larger horizon. That's the central thesis in this primer.

Moral philosophers may point out that any study of evil, however carefully crafted, contains a moral philosophy (just as Hans Kippenberg remarks that there is no history of religion that is not also a philosophy of religion).[15] I accept this, without conceding that a scholarly study of discourses on evil as dangers and aversions succumbs to the charge of blind moralism at a deeper level. Because this is a critical primer and not a philosophical treatise, my treatment of evil in relation to dangers and aversions focuses on a *functional* feature of morality. Morality, as Jürgen Habermas points out, is a social safety net (this would be my deeper level). If morality is protective, much like a register of health and harm, then dangers and aversions are central for understanding this contouring of human interaction. Studying evil by way of dangers and aversions sheds light on how we construct social systems using a wide range of protections and prohibitions to guide our norms and practices.

Before proceeding, it may be helpful to say a few things about the location of this project. In my view, the philosophy of evil has entered a labyrinth. For those familiar with the roads of Winnipeg, Manitoba, we could say that the philosophy of evil is like tragically navigating Confusion Corner, an intersection that might well have been designed by H. P. Lovecraft.[16] Confusion about evil is apparent when the concept is projected into archaic worldviews and simultaneously assumed to be thoroughly modern. In Nathan Loewen's words, it's no wonder that philosophers of evil conclude their work with "inscrutability, puzzlement, and the disruption of comprehension."[17] When

---

15. Hans G. Kippenberg, *Discovering Religious History in the Modern Age*, trans. Barbara Harshaw (Princeton, NJ: Princeton University Press, 2002), 1.

16. Retrieved October 6, 2021, from https://en.wikipedia.org/wiki/Confusion_Corner.

17. Loewen, *Beyond the Problem of Evil*, 128.

I read many of these books on evil, I feel as though I'm trapped in an endless maze of undesirable directions.

However, when we assume that the imagining of evil is shaped by a vast array of discourses seemingly unrelated to its focus—notions such as "clean" and "dirty" or "sacred" and "profane" for example—a larger horizon emerges. My proposal to study evil with an experimental framework comes out of a desire to broaden the horizon. I seek to explore what's missing from these debates, and what follows is a primer that introduces a familiar concept but that aims to see it anew. Built into this study are several commitments and contexts. My theoretical assumptions or inspirations are not raised as items for debate, since I will make no attempt to justify them. Rather, they are listed as ingredient labels for the cooking techniques used in this study.

First and foremost, this study is indebted to the critical social theory of Jürgen Habermas and his collaborators. Throughout the study, I assume the general accuracy of Habermas's theory of communicative action and communicative rationality.[18] I take from Habermas an interest in how human relationships are organized and how power influences decision making processes. Habermas's critique of metaphysics has also been invaluable for my attempts to think about evil differently.[19] In practical terms, the critique of metaphysics situates

---

18. For Habermas, communicative action concerns the consensual organization of human activity. Communicative rationality refers to the reasoning process underlying consensus oriented actions. On the priority of intersubjectivity and culture, see also Philippe Rochat, *Others in Mind* (Cambridge: Cambridge University Press, 2009) and Michael Tomasello, *The Cultural Origins of Human Cognition* (Cambridge, MA: Harvard University Press, 2009) and *Origins of Human Communication* (Cambridge, MA: MIT Press, 2010).

19. Jürgen Habermas, *Postmetaphysical Thinking: Philosophical Essays*, trans. William Mark Hohengarten (Cambridge, MA: MIT Press, 1992). In brief, Habermas argues that metaphysical claims rely on indeterminate premises, indelibly linked to unthematized circumstances and contexts. Postmetaphysical thinking seeks to uncouple claims from their contexts by means of linguistification, a communicative process that increases the comprehensibility of a claim by way of generalization and abstraction. In Habermas, the moral point of view, for example, must be formulated with sufficient abstraction to avoid the charge of particularism.

the human use of reason in history. At the same time, this critique resists assertions that privilege personal experience or cultural context and has the aim of creating openings for new conversations and new partners in conversation. The discourse on evil desperately needs new partners in conversation. I also share with Habermas and his colleagues an interest in the project of postmetaphysical thinking and communicative ethics. Taken together, these terms refer less to decisions about right and wrong and more to about how we arrive at those decisions. In the context of discourses on evil, many of the concerns discussed in María Pía Lara's anthology *Rethinking Evil* resonate with my aims.[20]

Second, this study is influenced by the work of several scholars working in or around the discipline of religion: Jonathan Z. Smith (comparison), Bruce Lincoln (power and authority), and Russell McCutcheon (mythmaking and social formation). The project has been crafted under the mentorship of *Guide to the Study of Religion*, edited by Willi Braun and Russell McCutcheon. I assume the importance of comparative analysis as an exemplary framework for studying and understanding human behavior and action. Also important are the works of Talal Asad, David Chidester, Hans Kippenberg, Tomoko Masuzawa, Brent Nongbri, and Aaron Hughes.[21] Since many of the scholars cited here advocate caution when using the word "religion," I'll simply note my conclusion on the topic. For the most

---

20. Edited by María Pía Lara (2001). See also Bernstein, *Radical Evil*; Peter Dews, *The Idea of Evil* (Malden, MA: Wiley-Blackwell, 2013); María Pía Lara, *Narrating Evil* (New York: Columbia University Press, 2007); and Martin Beck Matuštík, *Radical Evil and the Scarcity of Hope* (Bloomington, IN: Indiana University Press, 2008).

21. Smith, *Imagining Religion*; Bruce Lincoln, *Discourse and the Construction of Society*, 2nd edition (Chicago, IL: University of Chicago Press, 2014); Russell T. McCutcheon, *Critics Not Caretakers* (Albany, NY: SUNY Press, 2001) and *The Discipline of Religion* (New York: Routledge, 2003); Willi Braun and Russell T. McCutcheon, eds., *Guide to the Study of Religion* (New York: Continuum, 2000); Talal Asad, *Genealogies of Religion* (Baltimore, MD: Johns Hopkins, 1993); David Chidester, *Empire of Religion* (Chicago, IL: Chicago University Press, 2014); Kippenberg, *Discovering Religious History in the Modern Age*; Tomoko Masuzawa, *The Invention of World Religions* (Chicago, IL: University of Chicago Press, 2005); Brent Nongbri, *Before Religion* (New Haven, CT: Yale University Press, 2013); and Hughes, *Comparison*.

part, "religion" is an unhelpful term when it comes to scholarship because it too easily leads scholars into bad habits of thought. If the term comes up here, I tend to think of religion less as a self-contained bundle of individualistic beliefs and more as a style of interaction with (imagined) others. Religion within this conception highlights our collective capacity to create imaginary social worlds and interact with imaginary agents. The study of religion using this definition would include the manipulation and contestation of imaginary worlds and agents through ritual exchange, the machinations of canonization, and the laying down of stipulations for acting in the world in a way that it is not. The scope of this definition is far broader and more encompassing than anything resembling the paradigm of world religions. I am aiming to follow the recommendations and insights of William Arnal, Maurice Bloch, Tanya Luhrmann, Russell McCutcheon, and Marjorie Taylor.[22]

Third, my work here has been influenced by several strands of feminist theory. In particular, the writings of Seyla Benhabib (political philosophy), Marsha Hewitt (critical theory), Darlene Juschka (semiotics of gender), and Randi Warne (engendering).[23] Without recognizing the pervasive influence of systems of sex/gender, we won't really be able to understand much of anything. This is because, as Warne shows, the category "religion," and perhaps by extension the category "evil," is implicitly coded as feminine insofar as the explan-

22. My hope is that this kind of extensive redefinition starts us thinking differently about how we clump things together. We need different clumps. William Arnal and Russell T. McCutcheon, *The Sacred Is the Profane* (Oxford: Oxford University Press, 2012); Maurice Bloch, *Essays on Cultural Transmission* (Oxford: Berg, 2005) and *In and Out of Each Other's Bodies* (Boulder, CO: Paradigm, 2013); Tanya M. Luhrmann, *When God Talks Back* (New York: Vintage, 2012); and Marjorie Taylor, ed., *The Oxford Handbook of the Development of Imagination* (Oxford: Oxford University Press, 2013).

23. Seyla Benhabib, *The Claims of Culture* (Princeton, NJ: Princeton University Press, 2002); Marsha A. Hewitt, *Critical Theory of Religion* (Minneapolis, MN: Fortress Press, 1999); Darlene M. Juschka, *Political Bodies/Body Politic* (Sheffield: Equinox, 2009); Randi R. Warne, "Gender," in Braun and McCutcheon, *Guide to the Study of Religion*, 140–154 and "(En)gendering Religious Studies," *Studies in Religion/Sciences Religieuses* 27, no. 4 (1998), 427–436.

atory theoretical mechanism is said to neutralize the partialities and prejudices of the objective scholar (coded masculine). We live and theorize in the shadow of gender hierarchies and dyads. The best we can do is to focus on how they work and refuse to let our attention to these pervasive systems of exclusion and distortion slide from view.

Fourth, my work is shaped by recent studies concerning the imagination, especially research on our capacities for mental time travel, the imagining of agency, make-believe, and pretend play. This is a much-neglected field of study when it comes to the study of religion and I highly recommend the works of Marjorie Taylor, Paul Harris, Kendall Walton, and Jerome and Dorothy Singer.[24] It is this body of work, focusing on how we live in imaginary worlds populated by imaginary entities, that makes Maurice Bloch's insights concerning the transcendental social plausible.

Fifth, many of the key categories here have been elaborated in relation or in conversation with the novel *Dracula*. In 1998 I was a Teaching Assistant for Darlene Juschka in a course that used *Dracula* as a pedagogical tool. I hope I've learned the lesson; the novel has been required reading in my class for the better part of two decades. The distinction between moral evil and religious evil first occurred to me in the context of this novel when the characters scrupulously set out to annihilate Count Dracula because of his status as an abomination rather than put him on trial for his crimes.

Sixth, and this cannot be overstated, this book comes out of the course RLGN 1440 Evil in World Religions that I have been teaching at the University of Manitoba since 2002. The readings, works cited, and the arguments advanced are entwined with the requirements and limitations of teaching an introductory course in a Department of Religion. The ethnographic citations and examples reflect this

---

24. Marjorie Taylor, *Imaginary Companions and the Children Who Create Them* (Oxford: Oxford University Press, 1999); Paul L. Harris, *Children and Imagination* (Malden, MA: Blackwell Publishers, 2000) and *Trusting What You're Told* (Cambridge, MA: Belknap, 2015); Kendall L. Walton, *Mimesis as Make-Believe* (Cambridge, MA: Harvard University Press, 1990); Dorothy G. Singer and Jerome L. Singer, *The House of Make-Believe* (Cambridge, MA: Harvard University Press, 1992). See also K. S. Rosengren, C. N. Johnson, and P. L. Harris, eds., *Imagining the Impossible* (Cambridge: Cambridge University Press, 2000).

particular location. RLGN 1440 Evil in World Religions is the reason for this critical primer.

Finally, a note on intellectual inspiration. Seyla Benhabib's *Situating the Self* (1990) and *The Claims of Culture* (2002) focus on political practices of exclusion and articulate an anti-essentialist conception of culture as contradictory and contested. Social life, in her view, is continuously negotiated and renegotiated. This fluid model of culture, where people are understood to recalibrate their vocabularies and their justifications for norms as a matter of course, has been indispensable for rethinking evil in culture. If I can pay homage to one last essay, it is Maurice Bloch's "Why Religion is Nothing Special but is Central."[25] Bloch calls on scholars to focus more on the role of the imagination in constituting our taking for granted realities and expands the scope of religion to include the invisible worlds of essentialized identities and status functions.

It should also be noted, much of the material cited in this volume is redescriptive and builds on already redescriptive scholarship. For example, James Watson's account of funerals in Cantonese society redescribes death pollution as participating in a clearly defined social hierarchy. Watson's conclusions would likely not be recognized by the villagers discussed, just as the discussions of the male or female villagers on funerals may not be recognized by priestly accounts of funeral practices which would be different still from the viewpoint of the corpse handlers and so on. My use of Watson's ethnographic research is an interpretation of his interpretation which rests on the multiple and contrary interpretations of his collaborators and informants, themselves interpreting... The upshot is that my use of the material cited in this book may have little or nothing to do with the intentions or stated aims of the authors.

Following on this point, I should say something about expertise. This kind of study and analysis leads one well outside one's areas of expertise on numerous occasions. I am somewhat comforted by Jonathan Smith's remark that no comparative historian of religion can be expected to be an expert in everything they study.[26] Still,

---

25. Bloch, *In and Out of Each Other's Bodies*, 23–40.
26. Smith, *Imagining Religion*, 155, fn. 115.

ineptitude is not a virtue when it comes to scholarship. In order to address this, I have adopted a strategy that befits my purpose. When drawing on ethnographic examples, with only a few exceptions, I use a single source. Smith's twofold emphasis on example and reception is sidestepped since this is not a work of comparative history but a proposal for future study. I make no claims regarding the veracity of the events cited in my examples and want to make explicit that my citations are not there to settle disputes about what really happened. My purpose is to illustrate, by means of comparison, a feature or characteristic of human activity and to introduce a topic of study and set out a proposal for a course of study for that topic. In this case, the topic is evil and the course of study includes a series of key categories illustrated with examples drawn from around the world. The eclecticism of my selections is the result of the alchemy of opportunism, personal interest, the expertise of colleagues, and student patience. It is my hope that the model I am proposing could be developed and revised with more depth, sophistication, and tenacity.

Chapter 1

Introducing Evil

Despite the apparent difficulty, providing a definition of evil is a relatively easy thing to do. For my purposes here, evil is framed by dangers and aversions. The more demanding task lies in explaining why this particular definition is used and not another.

Like any other framing, mine invites questions about scale and scope. Doesn't this frame include too much? What gets to count as dangerous? Who gets to decide what counts? With so many dangers and aversions, hasn't this opened the door a little too wide? Should we paint humanitarian atrocities and food allergies with the same brush stroke? These are important questions and, by the end of this volume, I hope they will be addressed or at least held in abeyance to some satisfaction.

The proposed definition of evil as dangers and aversions is broad by design in order to dislodge our everyday assumptions about evil without leaving the field altogether. Maybe we can agree with Jonathan Z. Smith's observation that "scholarly labor is a disciplined exaggeration in the direction of knowledge."[1] The proposed definition is a conscientious and perhaps overly vigorous reminder that we are not dealing with a natural object but a category created and maintained by human interests.[2] Definitions establish a disciplinary

---

1. Smith, *Relating Religion*, 175.
2. By analogy, much of what I find problematic in studies on evil is exemplified by a remark made by Robert Segal about myth: "Theories need myths as much as myths need theories." This statement assumes a phenomenal existence of myth that then needs theoretical interpretation. This is precisely the problem. Evil doesn't need theories of evil to interpret or explain it. Theories of evil—folk theories, philosophical or theological theories, moral theories—create evil as a taxonomic category in the first place. Evil, myth, and religion are conceptual

horizon and provide contours for what is to be explored.[3] When defining evil as dangers and aversions what we call evil ranges from excessive salt consumption and crowded hallways to natural disasters and homicide. The enormity of the category is at once an advantage and a disadvantage. All of a sudden, evil is everywhere. There is an explosion of data. This is helpful because this definition opens our eyes to something interesting. Human beings avoid all sorts of things. And, I would argue, some of these things are treated with far more cruelty and contempt than the stuff we typically identify as evil.[4] Would you rather sit next to a well-dressed serial killer or someone who had just vomited in their lap? No one wants a drop of sewage in their glass of wine but we are perfectly willing to pump it into our rivers.

When viewed this way, the more common definition of evil, often associated with atrocity and the dismantling of humanity, looks embarrassingly slight. By the same token you might say, "I avoided a phone call from my employer ... so my employer is evil?" Yes. In this heuristic context, the purview of evil is immense. Anything we deem to be dangerous or that we avoid constitutes what will serve as the data for things that get labeled as evil, at least between the pages of this book. The definition is proposed as an experimental primer. The primer introduces the interplay of key categories and the insights of comparison. The experiment opens our eyes to a much wider array of human attitudes and practices that are relevant to the more familiar use of the term evil but that often go excluded or ignored.

For example, few people openly oppose or contest the idea that racist and sexist attitudes and practices exhibit clear affronts and violations to human rights and human dignity. While we might agree

constructs. Theories create their data as much as they describe or explain whatever they create. Segal, *Myth: A Very Short Introduction*, 2nd edition (Oxford: Oxford University Press, 2015), 9.

3. Smith, *Relating Religion*, 194.

4. Mary Jane Logan McCallum and Adele Perry capture aspects of this in their account of Brian Sinclair's death in the emergency room of a hospital in Winnipeg (September 2008). Brian Sinclair was "ignored to death" over a period of thirty-four hours in full view of staff and patients. McCallum and Perry, *Structures of Indifference: An Indigenous Life and Death in a Canadian City* (Winnipeg: University of Manitoba Press, 2018).

that racism and sexism are wrong, we must also ask about the attitudes and practices that instigate and make these offences possible. Most people agree that in order to change racist and sexist institutions and attitudes, we have to understand where they come from and how they work. This understanding is essential. However, how do we recognize when we are missing something? What prompts us not to see the obvious? How can we begin to see something hidden in plain sight? When scholars have focused on racism and sexism, many have focused on individual intent and motivation, ignoring or failing to notice enabling social conditions. What are the social factors that play into categories of race and racialization or sex and gendering that don't appear to be relevant? How do we make these connections?

The course of study proposed here offers some tools for doing precisely this. This particular lens allows us to make connections between dangers and aversions in the broadest sense as well as the more intensive channeling of these attitudes and practices into elements of what we find in more traditional discourses on evil. In other words, I am proposing to focus on key elements of human interaction that are at work in how we shape and frame dangers and aversions with the aim of shifting our categories into a new configuration. It is one thing to provide a moral justification for opposition to racism and sexism with an appeal to moral laws or human rights; it is another thing to provide a framework for better understanding how it is that race and sex are conceivable in the first place and recognize how these kind of discourses about race and sex draw on other less obvious discourses for coalescing their power and authority. How does an emotion such as disgust, for instance, wittingly or unwittingly contribute to our judgments about good and bad, desirable and undesirable? What are the ingredients that foster contempt and social distancing in this instance and not another?

This is not the only way to proceed. Another viable path would be to trace a genealogy of discourses on evil and their attending politics. As mentioned in the Preface, I leave that to others.[5] My aims here are in line with the interests of social anthropology and comparative religion. The genealogical approach requires an intensive study of

---

5. See, for example, the excellent study by Loewen, *Beyond the Problem of Evil*.

the social history of the discourse. While this would surely show us something about the politics of evil and the assumptions and exclusions of the current systems of classification, it would not address the analogous, the discourses and practices that function similarly but are not semantically or genealogically related to the discourse on evil. Focusing on dangers and aversions as a framework for reimagining evil aims to be inclusive of both the genealogy of the discourse on evil as well as its possible analogues. Through use of a critical primer, I hope to shed light on a range of human practices and discourses that exhibit similar patterns of interaction but are also quite different in terms of their function and context. To this end, we'll be working with some rather abstract categories and risking a bit of speculation about what cross-cultural analysis and comparison can tell us about how we imagine and regulate human interactions.

I think there is good reason to expand the topic in this way, even if this framing comes with some rather clumsy baggage. The point of a definition is to create contours. The fences we create are maintained by a sense of purpose. Our purpose is to expand the horizon with the aim of identifying a range of human interactions that can be used to inform the more traditional discourses on evil. My hope is that this kind of comparative approach will produce some sort of surprise which then prompts renewed efforts of interpretation and explanation and possibly the adjustment of categories or basic concepts.[6]

As mentioned, the purpose here is expressed with deceptive simplicity. We're here to study evil, defined as the study of dangers and aversions, in order to better understand and situate discourses on evil commonly found in moral philosophy in a cross-cultural context. It is a second-order experiment designed to clarify our first order commitments, assumptions, prejudices, and intuitions. This critical primer introduces the reader to some basic categories and a handful of illustrations. It is a field guide for identifying dangers and aversions in the wild. In the end, it should allow us to encounter the study of evil with a fresh perspective.

One of the reasons for this approach can be illustrated with a piece of personal narrative. My encounter with evil as a topic of study

---

6. Smith, *Relating Religion*, 175.

began with the question of theodicy (God and evil) at the University of Windsor, where I was an undergraduate in Religious Studies in the early 1990s. I was very intently introduced to a solution to the "problem of evil" in the form of something called process theology. Process theologians wrap theodicy in a mystical blanket and enjoin us to find consolation in the fact that God is somehow here and there even when evil strikes. As a graduate student at the University of Toronto, I remained interested in theodicy, although I was becoming increasingly aware of the chasm between theology and the study of religion.[7] As I came to know the writings of critical thinkers including Feuerbach, Marx, Adorno, and Habermas, more and more the theological options appeared as little more than thinly veiled conceit and thus no option at all.

I became especially mindful of the practical character of this conceit when I submitted a research paper proposing a postmetaphysical critique of theodicy to my theodicy professor (pretty much every religion department has someone who teaches a class on evil and religion). The paper was rejected as off-topic, and I was tasked with writing a second paper. The second research paper I wrote for the class was accepted but written off as insincere, since I had taken umbrage with the assumptions made by the scholars listed in the required readings. My intellectual frustration and labor had earned a solid B+ with the accompanying comment that I needed to take my studies more seriously. Perhaps this was a warning about the dangers of critical thinking?

Throughout this time, as best as I can recall, no one ever treated the historical context of the scholars writing about theodicy as the more interesting source of data.[8] Instead of asking about the social conditions that fostered evil as a topic, the relevance and significance of evil as something true and real was simply assumed. An operating

---

7. Donald Wiebe, *The Irony of Theology and the Nature of Religious Thought* (Montréal: McGill-Queen's University Press, 1991) and *The Politics of Religious Studies* (New York: Palgrave, 1999).

8. I was delighted to read McCutcheon, "'Like Small Bumps on the Back of the Neck ...': The Problem of Evil as Something Ordinary," *The Discipline of Religion* (New York: Routledge, 2003), 146–166.

assumption of most theodicies is the universality of the theodicy question itself. This assumption manages to remain relatively unreflected upon even when theodicy steps out of a monotheistic context and into an encounter with world religions.[9] Most scholars writing about theodicy simply assume that everyone everywhere has roughly the same sort of problem with something called evil.

After years of being ensnared in the problem of evil as managed by theodicies, my first inkling of a more productive approach was found in Mary Douglas's *Purity and Danger* (1966).[10] Her remarkable study addresses the universality of pollution and prohibition. If pollution regulations are not universal, they certainly exhibit strong cross-cultural tendencies. Douglas argues that human beings excel at coordinating their actions by creating shared systems of meaning. In her approach, which starts with reflections on dirt and hygiene, I began to see a way of approaching the topic of evil without strong assumptions about what evil is. Dirt is "matter out of place." It does not belong, and we eliminate it as a matter of course. Evil, however, has a place within our hierarchy of norms and values when we suggest that there's good and there's evil. However much we have learned to identify and abhor whatever is classified as evil, we give it a place. By way of contrast, dirt has no home, and removing dirt is

---

9. The bizarreness of this encounter should not be lost on us. What emerges as a logical problem within a particular branch of Christian theology is transformed, without so much as a nod or a blush, into a crisis of global proportions for all people. The strangeness of the universalizing of a Christian theological debate is very reminiscent of the maneuvering of Ernst Troesltch, especially as discussed by Masuzawa in *The Invention of World Religions*, 309–328. For some strange encounters with evil, suffering, and world religions see William Cenkner, ed., *Evil and the Response of World Religion* (St. Paul's, MN: Paragon House, 1997); and John Bowker, *Problems of Suffering in Religions of the World* (Cambridge: Cambridge University Press, 1970).

10. Although I had briefly encountered Douglas's work in graduate school, I hadn't grasped its relevance until cited in Paul Ricoeur's *The Symbolism of Evil*, trans. Emerson Buchanan (Boston, MA: Beacon Press, 1969). While I find Ricoeur's work fascinating, it too easily participates in the very problem I was seeking to work through.

little more than organizing the environment for the things that have a place in this world.

Focusing on human beings as classificatory creatures, Douglas sees the relation between order and disorder as a complex relation of interpretation, risk, and power. Separating, classifying, and cleansing are positive efforts, creative movements in our making sense of the world. Prohibitions protect and shore up established categories, as well as provide opportunities for challenging them. When uncertainty strikes, prohibitions can be used to pivot ambiguity into one sphere or another (clean or dirty, sacred or profane, relevant or irrelevant). At the same time, ritual play often makes use of the articulate and inarticulate. There is power in disorder as much as there is danger. Risks and dangers adhere along the edges of prohibitions that can be shifted when opportunities arise.[11] This is one of the reasons why Douglas's work is so important. When we give evil a place we often forget or ignore the social interests profiting from its placement. When we eliminate dirt, we don't think twice about it.

Another innovation of Douglas's approach to purity and danger is that it abolishes the popular nineteenth-century distinction between "primitive superstition" and "scientific hygiene." In the nineteenth century, many anthropologists made much of a distinction between primitives and moderns: "they" have superstition and religion while "we" have hygiene and science. Douglas argues that the difference becomes a matter of degree, not of kind. Clean and dirty represent the work of classification, not civilizational hierarchy. As creatures of classification, demarcating and naming the world is an unavoidable aspect of cognition and cooperative action. Dirt has no home, but it is always with us because our schemas have boundaries. Around the edges and between the cracks, we have dirt, and with dirt, we have dangers. This is a source of great risk and perhaps great power. Focusing on the cracks and crevices seems like a sensible place to start a course on the study of evil.

The strategic difference between Douglas's understanding of risk and prohibition and my conception of dangers and aversions concerns the aims of our respective projects. *Purity and Danger* is a book

---

11. Mary Douglas, *Purity and Danger* (New York: Routledge, 2002), 117–140.

about order and disorder. More precisely, about the ordering of dis-order. She identifies purity, contagion, and prohibition as universal features of human society. Alternatively, my emphasis on dangers and aversions is in the service of a suspicion that our discourses on evil are impoverished and could be enriched by engaging with an enlarged account of human interaction.

As a way of introducing students to the cracks and crevices and the displacement of moving from a personal idea about evil to a second-order conception of evil as dangers and aversions, I often began my first class by eating a potato chip off the floor. I'd start by asking, "How many of you would like to have a religious experience?" I then placed a chip on the floor, counted to five, and proceeded to eat it. Most of the time there was an audible gasp. In the discussion following the transgression of edible etiquette, no one ever suggested that eating a chip from the floor was evil. However, most agreed that it was dangerous. Once the chip touched the floor it was transformed from junk food into true garbage, with all the negative associations we have with refuse and waste.[12]

The keen insights of Douglas are made possible by comparisons between purity and impurity, order and disorder, clean and dirty. When drawn into the orbit of the topic of evil, her work suggests that, if we look past a strictly moralist conception of evil to inter-actions with a broader basis in natural history, such as elementary avoidances or the classification of dangers, we'll see something new. Douglas's work affords us an opportunity to redefine evil for the pur-pose of studying attitudes and practices that run alongside contem-porary discourses on evil but are ignored or dismissed as irrelevant (if even noticed). I think this is a desirable outcome. I have no wish to abandon the moral or philosophical topic of evil. However, moral philosophy will be better with a stronger self-awareness about the range of attitudes and practices that inform moral judgments as well as the more discrete attitudes and practices work as silent partners. We might not say that dirt is evil, but whatever we classify as dirty

---

12. I performed this stunt for several years but stopped after the room I was teaching in was treated for asbestos removal. Sometimes we end up falling into our own theories.

can be removed without much question or consideration. Keeping the streets clean refers to a lot more than sweeping up debris.

Embedded within discourses about dirt and dangers are a variety of social interests, strategies, and operating assumptions regarding highly localized shared social imaginaries—including attractions, estrangements, and contradictions. Taxonomies, for instance, may create, maintain, or dissolve social hierarchies.[13] Bruce Lincoln's essay "The Tyranny of Taxonomy" is introduced with an example of how seating arrangements at the dining room table of his childhood reflect a four-part hierarchic set based on age (adults/children) and gender (male/female). The placement of people reflects status and authority. Extending the discussion, Lincoln observes that these arrangements are "instruments for the organization of society" where seemingly innocuous social groupings are treated as instances of a general cosmic law. When changes are made to social groupings, around notions such as "pure" or "impure," the displacement of authority, either upward or downward, may be justified or naturalized as cosmic judgements rather than viewed as reflections of cloaked group interests.[14]

Given that conceptions of dirt and danger are contextually and linguistically embedded, we should not expect to find shared practices or norms across cultures. We can't even expect consistency or stability within a single location. My requirements for a clean coffee mug at home are different from my requirements for a clean coffee mug in a restaurant. Dirt may be useful as a cross-cultural analytic concept, but every instance of dirt avoidance will be unique (in an ordinary way).

For example, one of my favorite in-class experiments runs a bit like this: I break the class into smaller groups and ask them to rank the places they would least like to eat a meal off the floor. They are given

---

13. Lincoln, *Discourse and the Construction of Society*, 1–10. See also Gary Lease, "Ideology," in Braun and McCutcheon, eds., *Guide to the Study of Religion* (New York: Continuum, 2000), 438–447; and McCutcheon, "Redescribing 'Religion' as Social Formation," *Critics Not Caretakers* (Albany, NY: State of New York Press, 2001), 21–39.

14. Lincoln, *Discourse and the Construction of Society*, 131–141.

the options: transit bus, gas station, gourmet coffee shop, hospital, and cafeteria. After the ranking we talk about the criteria used for their rankings excluding considerations of hygiene. In most groups it turns out that accessibility and traffic are the determining ingredients. In this highly anecdotal account, exclusivity seems to correlate with associations of cleanliness.

These contextual limitations of dirt work well as a starting point. We will examine several instances of dangers and aversions as they might be redescribed using features of the key categories. The aim is to draft a sketch of the vicissitudes of dangers and aversions with a gesture towards their relevance for better understanding discourses on evil, prompting us to reconsider what we talk about when we talk about evil. This study is fashioned not as a work of comparative history, but as a primer for further reading in comparative history. It should also be useful in setting the stage for more textured discussions in moral philosophy. Dangers and aversions are found across cultures and throughout our natural history. This is a theoretical assumption, for better and worse. With dangers and aversions serving as the shared common ground between items of comparison, we then have a framework for comparison. We see that, despite the ubiquity of dangers and aversions, they are identified and categorized and responded to quite differently.[15] We begin to see not only contrasting imaginings of dangers and aversions but also different mechanisms for generating them.

Dangers and aversions are identifiable on the level of behavior and on the level of social action and coordination. What constitutes dangers and aversions varies widely (as does what constitutes health and harm). However, there are strong cross-cultural patterns in human interactions. The proposed key categories in relation to evil give names to these patterns. In general, human beings avoid pain, although in some instances we seek it. We tend to avoid noxious

---

15. "Comparison is, at base, never identity. Comparison requires the postulation of difference as the grounds of its being interesting (rather than tautological) and a methodical manipulation of difference, a playing across the 'gap' in the service of some useful end." Jonathan Z. Smith, "In Comparison Magic Dwells," *Imagining Religion* (Chicago, IL: University of Chicago Press, 1982), 35.

smells, although sometimes we seek them out with great affection. Often enough, human beings identify the feminine as secondary to the masculine, even when the creator of Wonder Woman tried to reverse this (with questionable results).[16] The advantage of defining evil as dangers and aversions is that it resonates broadly within much of the literature I've encountered in the course of my studies in the discipline of religion. While the domain of dangers and aversions is as unwieldy as it is vast, limits are reached in the selection of exemplars. The scope of the definition is circumscribed by decisions about the examples that enliven these concepts.

So why frame "evil" as dangerous and aversions? Why not simply retitle the book *Dangers: A Critical Primer*? To be blunt, I think the evil industry is heading in the wrong direction. It seems to me that it is too easy to claim that evil is either a human problem that we must continually attempt to wrestle with or that evil is a non-problem that we can simply ignore because there's no such thing. I want scholars writing about evil to rethink the topic, and I want teachers and students to encounter the topic differently than we have in the past. Instead of starting with evil as a universal problem, I want teachers and students to start with questions about how we come to think about something *as* evil in the first place. Instead of asking, "What is evil?", we might instead ask about how we go from ordinary aversion (avoiding people) to human atrocity (ignoring people to death)? Once we understand and map the terrain of dangers and aversions, we'll be better poised to think about how the intensification of dangers and aversions engineers us to recognize something as evil. We will also be able to recognize certain kinds of action having to do with dangers and aversions as producing social formations of exclusion, hierarchy, marginalization. Once we better understand the scope and function of danger, we'll be in a better position to think about how human beings collectively respond to a variety of events and circumstances, even if at first some of these appear nondescript or irrelevant. My

---

16. By way of contrast, I think the Ms. Marvel of G. Willow Wilson is the more interesting superhero. See Jessica Baldanzi and Hussein Rashid, eds., *Ms. Marvel's America: No Normal* (Jackson, MS: University Press of Mississippi, 2020).

hope in all this is to lay some groundwork and basic concepts for recalibrating the study of evil.

Why is this definition better than competing definitions? Why not start with ethics or law? This is a question that can't really be answered in a straightforward way. On the one hand, it isn't better. There is no such thing as a true or false definition. Definitions are more or less useful for understanding something. On the other hand, the utility of a definition must prove itself in the long run. Utility is not established in a single experiment. What can we hope to gain by defining evil this way? My aim is to treat something deemed indescribable as something ordinary, to redescribe it in a way that sheds light on discernable social patterns. At the end of the experiment, will things appear differently? The question is prompted by a degree of dissatisfaction with existing studies on the topic of evil found in moral philosophy.[17] The definition is animated by questions such as: what makes evil thinkable? What makes the concept attractive? What underlies the idea of evil, and what words we might use if we were to describe it differently?

Conceptually, defining evil as dangers and aversions is linked to Jürgen Habermas's comments regarding the relation between protective norms and harm: "In anthropological terms, morality is a safety device compensating for a vulnerability built into the sociocultural form of life."[18] While health and harm inform morality, a wider net of dangers and aversions may be associated with health and harm, but not always. For instance, not all things to be avoided are damaging. We often avoid things because they are inconvenient. Evil as dangers and aversions includes ordinary avoidances, perceived or interpreted as harmful or not. This panoramic definition is inspired both

---

17. I am especially dissatisfied with moral philosophers who suggest events in human history are ineffable or unspeakable. This kind of talk imposes a mystifying transcendent framework on something that, even if hard to grasp, remains human. See Naomi Mandel, "Rethinking 'After Auschwitz': Against a Rhetoric of the Unspeakable in Holocaust Writing," *Boundary 2* 28, no. 2 (2001), 203–228. Many thanks to the anonymous reader who drew attention to my use of "moral philosophers" as antagonists as well as making explicit why I've done so.

18. Habermas, *Moral Consciousness and Communicative Action*, trans. Christian Lenhardt and Shierry Weber Nicholsen (Cambridge, MA: MIT Press, 1990), 199.

by Habermas's understanding of morality as protective and Douglas's understanding that risk and prohibition engage and protect a vision of the communal good life.[19] Rethinking evil as dangers and aversions may facilitate new ways of thinking about the cognitive and cultural foundations of morality and ethics—foundations rooted in a wider range of human practices and discourses than typically thought.

As intended, the definition provided allows us to study evil as a socially constructed object. We're not going to decide what is right and wrong here. From the perspective advanced, evil is circumscribed artificially for the purposes of explanation, comparison, and understanding. It is a definition that belongs to this particular study and is a function of the interests invoked. Next time, the definition will be different because we will have learned something about dangers and aversions in a cross-cultural context. Once we have a better sense of how dangers and aversions are constructed, we'll revise the terms of our study and take a different step. In constructing our study in this way we are avoiding the first-order question of what evil is by adopting a second-order perspective. In order to illustrate the difference between a participatory or first-person conception of evil and an objectivating conception of evil, we can look to the difference between Richard J. Bernstein's *Radical Evil* and David Frankfurter's *Evil Incarnate*.

Richard Bernstein's *Radical Evil* is an excellent example of a participatory approach to evil. For Bernstein, evil is not something that can be defined once and for all. Instead, it is experienced as a presence and we are compelled to respond. Complete comprehension of evil is impossible. The task of the philosopher is an ongoing interrogation of evil, a series of pragmatic and dialogical interpretations and engagements. In his Introduction to the book, Bernstein expresses skepticism towards the possibility of developing a theory of evil at all.[20] Bernstein's approach is practical, in that it aims to come to terms

---

19. "If risk and taboo turnout to be equally engaged in protecting a vision of the good community, whether it is a vision of stable continuity or of sustained radical challenge, I will have achieved my original intention." Douglas, *Purity and Danger*, xx.

20. Bernstein, *Radical Evil*, 6–7.

with the painful incongruities of atrocity. His study is an extensive engagement with a philosophical tradition that begins with Kant and moves through Hegel, Schelling, Nietzsche, Freud, Levinas, Jonas, and Arendt.

Discussing evil in a very different way, David Frankfurter's *Evil Incarnate: Rumors of Demonic Conspiracy and Satanic Abuse in History* examines how human beings conceptualize evil, providing a study of the rhetoric and the power of rhetoric to inform social actions. Frankfurter registers how "images of evil can develop in the cultural imagination" and examines the cultural construction of evil drawing on a series of case studies.[21] Frankfurter's study includes sections on demonologies, curators and purveyors of demonologies, and the rituals, rhetoric, and myths of evil. His work concludes that those involved in lynching, witch-burning, and genocide "understand themselves not to be doing evil but rather to be cleansing their communities from evil: monstrous, pernicious evil."[22]

Defining evil as dangers and aversions is sympathetic to Frankfurter's historical and comparative approach. At the same time, it also participates in what Bernstein calls an "interrogation of evil." My proposal here works with and within existing philosophical debates but is also amenable to and implicated in historical, ethnographic, and comparative research. In other words, I'm not drawing a definition of evil out of a recipe box at random. Informed by a range of works from history and cultural anthropology to critical theory and discourse ethics, my decision is motivated by existing discourses, but steps back from them. I'm looking not only for what they have in common but also for a more comprehensive rubric that facilities or invites cross-cultural and critical comparison. I pay tribute to the canon of moral philosophy but, at the same time, situate that canon in the service of questions asked by a dissatisfied scholar of religion.

Each of the following chapters introduces a key category important to this reconsideration of evil. Chapter 2 introduces the first two concepts: **classification** and **magical thinking**. Classification refers to how we make sense of the world by creating definitions, boundaries,

---

21. Frankfurter, *Evil Incarnate*, xiii.
22. Frankfurter, *Evil Incarnate*, 224.

and hierarchies. Magical thinking is a kind of essence-attributing cognition that makes designations stick. The chapter places Mary Douglas's anthropological conception of classification alongside a conception of magical thinking developed within psychology. I illustrate magical thinking with reference to three examples of dangers and aversions: death pollution, germs and gentility, and abomination.

Chapter 3 offers a discussion of the third concept, **ritual**, by drawing heavily on Maurice Bloch's classic essay on formalization. For Bloch, religious ritual is an extreme example of the power and authority of highly formalized relations. I cite three examples, each illustrating a different kind of authorization: the creation of authority (witnessing), the maintaining of authority (daily prayers), and the dissolving of authority (profane exhumations).

After an analysis of ritual, I take up **myth** and mythmaking in Chapter 4. As developed by Russell McCutcheon, myth is a form of meaning-making that encompasses the maneuvering of normative systems of classification. To elaborate on this in connection to dangers and aversions, I again turn to three examples: storytelling about the devil, narratives about the ideals of womanhood, and overlapping systems of androcentrism.

Chapter 5 introduces **strong emotions** as another key category related to dangers and aversions. Specifically, I examine the emotions shame and disgust, each with a single case study to illustrate dangers and aversions in the context of sex, gender, and sexuality. Sex/gender systems are codified systems that register dangers and aversions, often in terms of (male) purity and (female) impurity. Since "the feminine" is often at heart of myths about pollution, it becomes necessary to recognize the androcentric interests at work in the politics of classifying dangers and aversions.

Finally, in Chapter 6, I introduce the category **morality** as a discourse through which dangers and aversions are refined and clarified. Moral discourse creates and recommends a procedure for adjudicating dangers and aversions with an emphasis on rights, agency, autonomy, and solidarity. What is curious about morality is its explicit critique of the ideological influences of magical thinking, ritual, myth, and strong emotions. In many respects, moral thought has been constructed as a means of dismantling the authorizations created by the previously mentioned conceptions. Important to note, morality is not used in a participatory way here. However much I agree or disagree with this conception of morality, the examples used show how morality, as a key category within a comparative analysis of dangers and aversion, is imagined as a deliberative and critical practice.

* * *

Throughout the chapters dealing with key categories, I've relied on a puzzle piece metaphor. Each key category is a piece of the puzzle that will create an incongruous picture of evil (as dangers and aversions). These pieces don't necessarily go together—the fit is itself an artifice. Maybe we can imagine a bag of jigsaw pieces from half a dozen puzzles, and we're sorting them out and putting them onto the floor. We're not sure which pieces belong to which puzzle, but we're going to work on it for the afternoon. In doing so, we're creating a composition with pieces from anthropology, psychology, the study of religion, and rhetoric. It may not be polished or finished, but it is crafted with intent. In the end, we will have created a picture using what we have on hand. Hopefully the fabricated image will give us insight into the fabricating process itself as much as it does the patterning of human dangers and aversions.

Chapter 2

Classification and Magical Thinking

When it comes to dangers and aversions, classification is a good place to start. Classification refers to how people carve up the world and make sense of things. According to anthropologist Mary Douglas, "the activity of classifying is a human universal" and is the means through which basic distinctions between order and chaos, known and unknown, are made.[1] Classification schemas do more than line up names and things: they prescribe behavior, create hierarchies and rankings, and, most relevantly here, register and catalogue dangers and aversions.[2] Classification systems establish what counts and doesn't count as reality alongside what is permissible and forbidden. Distinctions between edible and inedible, living and dead, animal and human, clean and dirty are all products of classification.

Schemes of classification are remarkably diverse across cultures, and, aside from being able to say that we are classificatory creatures, there doesn't seem to be much in common when it comes to the particulars. Despite the range of variance, Douglas proposes that there are discernable cross-cultural patterns in how symbol systems work when it comes to classification. Specifically, there is a tendency to create meaning close to our embodied experiences, and many of our dangers and aversions relate to the regulation of the body. As Darlene Juschka puts it, the body is the "primary site for the struggle between heaven and earth," and all sorts of powers of governance register their power by means of encoding the body in myth and ritual.[3] This means that we should not be surprised to find cross-cultural affinities when it comes to the regulation of the body (and body politic).

---

1. Douglas, *Purity and Danger*, xvii.
2. Douglas, *Purity and Danger*, 5.
3. Juschka, *Political Bodies/Body Politic*, 97.

While systems of classification may vary widely, we will find common themes—clean and dirty, for example. When it comes to purity and impurity, as Douglas observes, death, food, identity, and sex are all products of classificatory regulation. Boundaries and hierarchies are built by dangers and aversions.

A useful illustration of hierarchies and classification can be made by considering the difference between natural vanillin and artificial vanillin. What we call vanilla is the spice derived from the seed pods of a vanilla orchid. Vanillin is the key component of the flavor we associate with vanilla. Vanillin has the molecular formula $C_8H_8O_3$. Artificial vanillin, with the same molecular formula, can be produced from petroleum, spruce tree lignin, rice bran, clove oil, and corn sugar. The result has created some interesting debates about what counts as "natural" and what counts as "artificial" or, more to the point, what can be *labeled* as natural vanilla extract versus artificial vanilla extract.[4] There's nothing unnatural about corn sugar, even if it has been manipulated into molecular vanillin, right? For some, however, only vanillin from the vanilla bean counts as real vanilla— even if the molecular formula produced by a synthetic process is identical. After informally presenting the matter to my students, a vast majority indicated that they would be willing to pay more for authentic vanillin when preparing a baked good for someone they love (although one of my more thrifty students remarked that they would purchase the synthetic version of vanilla because if the person truly loved them back, they would understand). While the question occurs in the context of chemistry and cuisine, it is clearly a matter of classification. Regardless of taste, whatever manages to find itself labelled as natural, pure, or authentic is often ranked higher in the grand order of things than the synthetic. From within a hierarchy of authentic and inauthentic, artificial vanillin finds itself on the side of

---

4. Havkin-Frenkel *et al.*, "A Comprehensive Study of Composition and Evaluation of Vanilla Extracts in US Retails Stores," *Handbook of Vanilla Science and Technology* (Malden, MA: Blackwell Publishing, 2011), 220–234 and Melody M. Bomgardner, "The Problem with Vanilla," *Chemical and Engineering News* 94, 36 (2016), retrieved June 24, 2021, from https://cen.acs.org/articles/94/i36/problem-vanilla.html.

the unnatural—it's just chemicals! We can see that authenticity is a complex ideological judgement about what counts as natural or even what counts as real. Authenticity, pure and impure, is a judgement that follows from classification.

In the context of our interest in dangers and aversions as a framework for thinking about evil, Douglas makes the critical point that material outside our systems of classification take the form of dirt: "matter out of place."[5] Dirt refers to all the stuff that doesn't quite fit our classifications:

> Dirt is essentially disorder. There is no such thing as absolute dirt: it exists in the eye of the beholder. If we shun dirt, it is not because of craven fear, still less dread of holy terror. Nor do our ideas about disease account for the range of our behavior in cleaning or avoiding dirt. Dirt offends against order. Eliminating it is not a negative movement, but a positive effort to organize the environment.[6]

According to Douglas, dirt is a byproduct of our systems of classification. Dirt is perceived as a threat to the symbolic order because it contradicts or offends our cherished categories.[7] Douglas argues that the chaos of "matter out of place" is often shunted into the realm of the sacred: if it doesn't fit, it is set apart and assigned extraordinary status. While Douglas argues that dirt is often made special, I would modestly suggest that dirt can be pivoted into any number of domains.[8] Her main point is that classification imposes order and prohibitions shore up and preserve ordering categories: "Ideas about separating, purifying, demarcating and punishing transgressions have as their main function to impose system on an inherently untidy experience."[9] Chaos, disorder, and dirt reside along the edges of our categories. Proximity to these edges is often thought to bring the possibility of contamination. Impurity is the work product of contradiction and conflicts between categories, insofar as they trouble

---

5. Douglas, *Purity and Danger*, 44.

6. Douglas, *Purity and Danger*, 2.

7. Douglas, *Purity and Danger*, xvii, 44–45.

8. Jonathan Z. Smith, "The Wobbling Pivot," *Map Is Not Territory* (Chicago, IL: University of Chicago Press, 1978).

9. Douglas, *Purity and Danger*, 5.

traditional boundaries. In Douglas's view, impurity harbors risks because of its connection to dirt. Such risks are as much the result of the untidy nature of existence as the imperfect nature of our categories. Around the edges, in the cracks, and through the contradictions, there be dragons ... and, it would appear, something called "evil."

A personal example might help demonstrate the point. While preparing something in the kitchen, I took a scoop of butter from the butter dish using a knife. I took too much and left the remainder on the tip of the knife and left the knife on the counter. With one thing leading to another, the knife remained on the counter with a patch of butter stacked on the tip until it was time to do dishes after the meal. Without really thinking about it, I washed the dishes, left the knife with the butter for later, and carried on with the evening. The next morning, in the cold light of day, the knife with an affixed patch of butter remained. Yesterday it seemed like perfectly usable butter. In the morning it was, as Douglas might have noted, "matter out of place." At some seemingly bewitched point between evening and morning, the buttered knife touched chaos. I was very tempted to purify the whole disorderly mess with some soap and hot water ... but what was the offense? The butter shouldn't be wasted. There's nothing wrong with the butter. And so, with all my training as a scholar of religion, I tried to regulate the contact with chaos by putting the butter on toast. Buttering toast seemed to be close enough to a purification ritual to satisfy my unsettled mind. Meanwhile, norms which had fallen lax in my distraction, were reasserted and reinforced: do the dishes, put food away.[10]

While penalties for deviance may be relatively minor, perhaps remedied by a simple ritual such as an apology or the washing of hands, there are instances when deviance comes at a much higher cost. Offenders who challenge or contradict the social order may find themselves on the wrong side of profanation and aligned with threats, not simply to the individual body but to the community and perhaps the world itself. Douglas provides an example of a group that views pregnancy as dangerous, not simply to the mother but to the

---

10. Andrea Brown further reminds me that the proper place for butter is also a contested classification: refrigerator or counter?

entire community. A fetus is seen as voracious and will consume or damage crops if brought near them.[11] And how many times have you heard a professor complain about the tragic condition of education today after marking a batch of papers where citations didn't comply with the dictates of the most recent edition of the style guide? In any grand schema, individual dangers and aversions may spread and threaten the entire cosmological system.

The ease with which categories can be threatened by contradiction makes untidy existence a perpetual problem for the maintenance of symbol systems. Etiquette, prohibitions, and traditions can be creatively deployed as a means of dealing with messy contingencies, but the ideal never quite matches up with the real.[12] Rather than be governed by a single authority people "pick, mix, and combine a variety of religious and cultural idioms."[13] Political and cultural upheavals threaten established categories. As our social ecosystems change, we change along with them, leaving our classification systems in disrepair and in need of constant maintenance.

For our purposes here, dirt serves as an excellent starting point for a discussion about evil when the latter is defined as dangers and aversions because of dirt's variance and intensity, as well as its capacity to slip under the radar of moral philosophy. As we saw in the example of vanillin, many debates about authenticity are framed in the language of hierarchy, preference, and aversion. With pollution anxieties, there is a tendency to focus on dangers—to the individual, the community, or the cosmos. Authenticity is often equated with purity, and purity is moralized and associated with "the good life" or a proper way of living.[14] Things that appear to threaten the integrity of so-called

---

11. Douglas, *Purity and Danger*, 119.

12. What might be referred to as the "religion of everyday social exchange." Stanley Stowers cited in Jennifer Eyl, "Religion Makes People Moral," in Brad Stoddard and Craig Martin, eds., *Stereotyping Religion: Critiquing Clichés* (New York: Bloomsbury, 2017), 47.

13. Sean McCloud, "Religions are Belief Systems," in Brad Stoddard and Craig Martin, eds., *Stereotyping Religion: Critiquing Clichés* (New York: Bloomsbury, 2017), 16.

14. For an excellent critique of a more philosophically developed understanding of authenticity, see Theodor W. Adorno, *The Jargon of Authenticity*, trans.

authentic categories are readily labelled as polluting or profaning elements within the larger array of symbols. This can be applied to synthetic flavoring or to interactions with other groups. We don't have to look too far into the history of "scholarship" on race, blood, and DNA to see this kind of thinking at work today.[15] It is important to reassert and clarify that dirt is not "evil" in the moral sense. Threats to traditional categories are often only perceived threats. We're talking about social worlds and shared fantasies. That said, responses will be varied. Dangers can be ignored or tolerated or even encouraged. Responses to pollution vary as well, of course. The consequences of pollution may be anything from a minor inconvenience to the marshaling of cosmic disaster.

It is also important to see that our categories often serve dual purposes: descriptive and prescriptive. When someone describes the proverbial elephant in the room, we ought to act as if there is an elephant in the room. The description gives way to prescription. In this way, classification systems reflect and encode larger cosmologies. They can also be used to reverse or modify these cosmologies.[16] Viewed in this way, we get a good sense of what Douglas means when she writes: "the whole universe is harnessed ... to force one another into good citizenship."[17] In such systems, as Douglas notes, the "laws of nature are dragged in to sanction the moral code," and if the laws of nature don't punish an offender, the neighbors certainly will.[18] A member of a believing community might receive extra visits from the faithful if their ritual obligations appear to be coming up short.

As should be evident, dirt is not necessarily the result of a concerted effort to demonize, although impurity can be treated in this way. As the byproduct of classification, dirt tends to participate in

---

Knut Tarnowski and Frederic Will (Evanston, IL: Northwestern University Press, 1973).

15. Kim Tallbear, *Native American DNA: Tribal Belongings and the False Promise of Genetic Science* (Minneapolis, MN: University of Minnesota Press, 2013), 31–66.

16. Almost anything and everything by Bruce Lincoln could be cited here. His overview of the topsy-turvy history of mythos and logos is a convenient example. Lincoln, *Theorizing Myth* (Chicago, IL: University of Chicago Press, 1999), 3–43.

17. Douglas, *Purity and Danger*, 4.

18. Douglas, *Purity and Danger*, 4.

dyadic positions: clean and dirty, order and disorder, sacred and profane, good and evil. While we can readily agree that classification is a
human universal, what makes certain categories stick? What makes
abstract symbol systems more tangible? Just how do people come to
agree on what to call dangerous? Questions about the durability of
our categories have longstanding histories across most disciplines
in the humanities and social sciences. In several of my classes, I raise
the issue this way: I hold up a bottle of water and ask, "How do we
turn this into something else? How about turning it into a queen in
a game of chess? How can we do that?" Students are often baffled for
a moment but catch on quickly. After a few moments, someone will
respond and say, "You play chess with it." And so I set up the game
with the water bottle as the queen, and in the process, the water
bottle becomes a bit less of a water bottle. Over time, the objective
characteristics of the water bottle may disappear completely so that
we only notice its symbolic characteristics.[19] You can just as easily get
to the arbitrariness and stickiness of our categories by asking, "What
makes today Wednesday?"[20]

Classification results in our identification of what is and isn't dangerous. But what makes symbol systems work? What underlies their
fascinating power? The next puzzle piece is rooted in social cognition
and has to do with our capacity for essentialism—our ability to posit
essences or efficacies within appearances. It is this power to imbue
things with an unseen essence, I think, that serves as the glue that
sticks our otherwise ephemeral categories to bodies of the living. As
will be shown, these imagined efficacies are also at the heart of a good
many dangers and aversions.

---

19. Just to mess with my students, I hold up the water bottle on the last day
of class and ask what it is. The inevitable pause is telling. Another quick example
is money. From a purely functional point of view, cash bills aren't all that useful,
except maybe as a decent bookmark. If you were stranded in a forest, however,
would you rather have a wallet full of cash or a good pair of hiking boots? My
thanks to Darlene Juschka for this example.

20. My thanks to Naomi Goldenberg for this example.

Sympathetic Magical Thinking

Psychologists Carol Nemeroff and Paul Rozin develop a theory of magical thinking to help us understand how our everyday cognition makes meaningful connections between people and things. Their conception is as much a proposal for ongoing empirical testing as it is a provisional explanation of their findings. Nemeroff and Rozin propose that classical conceptions of magical thinking can be reworked and salvaged to better understand an extremely common and cross-cultural mode of cognition.[21] I introduce their work here and place it alongside several examples because a theory of sympathetic magical thinking provides insight into a dynamic of many classificatory practices, but certainly those identifying dangers and aversions.

Sympathetic magical thinking involves the positing of a "driving force, or essence, that travels along the lines determined by sympathy."[22] As outlined in Nemeroff and Rozin, it has two basic principles: the law of similarity (homeopathic magic) and the law of contagion

---

21. Classical conceptions of magic include the works of Tylor, Frazer, Mauss, Durkheim, Levy-Bruhl, and Malinowski. Nemeroff and Rozin's conception of magical thinking focuses on sympathetic magical thinking and should be understood as a subset of a more comprehensive theory of magical thinking. For a wider view of magical thinking, see the overview in Karl S. Rosengren and Jason A. French, "Magical Thinking," in M. Taylor, ed., *The Oxford Handbook of the Development of Imagination* (Oxford: Oxford University Press, 2013), 42–60 as well as Eugene Subbotsky, *Magic and the Mind: Mechanisms, Functions, and Development of Magical Thinking and Behavior* (Oxford: Oxford University Press, 2010). For some critical consideration about magical thinking and comparison, see Jonathan Z. Smith, "In Comparison a Magic Dwells," *Imagining Religion* (Chicago, IL: University of Chicago Press, 1982).

22. Carol Nemeroff and Paul Rozin, "The Makings of the Magical Mind: The Nature and Function of Sympathetic Magical Thinking," in Karl S. Rosengren, Carl N. Johnson, and Paul L. Harris, eds., *Imagining the Impossible: Magical, Scientific, and Religious Thinking in Children* (Cambridge: Cambridge University Press, 2000), 3. Nemeroff and Rozin describe this essence as "mana." Because of the complex colonial history of the term mana in the study of religion, I opt for the words essence or efficacy.

(contagious magic).[23] Abstracted from particular instances, the theory of magical thinking proposes that essentializing cognition, the thought process that imbues people and things with an invisible essence, is a basic and universal feature of human thought. Both magical laws involve the creative positing of a socially effective essence or efficacy and the connection of that essence with a person or thing. This efficacious identity is frequently imagined as being shared across time and space and often remains impervious to or separate from empirical observations.

The law of similarity "rests on the premise that things that resemble one another at a superficial level also share deeper properties."[24] The photograph of someone you love that you keep with you at all times is an example of this. The loved one and the image of the loved one are magically thought to share the same essence and are posited as having an essential or sympathetic affinity. An affront to the image is little different than an affront to the person represented in the image. Rozin and colleagues tested this with assorted replicas and photographs. They found that replicas of disgusting objects, such as rubber vomit, are often treated with the same regard that one would treat the disgusting object itself (actual vomit). A similar correspondence in attitude and behavior was found with photographs. Participants had a much harder time throwing darts at images of people they felt an affinity with. Perhaps the most striking example cited by Nemeroff and Rozin is that of an experiment where they affixed the label "cyanide" on a glass of sugared water. Despite knowing the water to be safe, participants in the study had a strong aversion to drinking it.[25]

In contrast to similarity, the law of contagion holds that "physical contact between the source and the target results in the transfer of some effect of quality (essence) from the source to the target."[26] The quality or valence of a contagious essence may be positive or

---

23. Nemeroff and Rozin posit a third principle, the law of opposition, which is a variant of the law of similarity.

24. Nemeroff and Rozin, "The Makings of the Magical Mind," 3.

25. Nemeroff and Rozin, "The Makings of the Magical Mind," 6.

26. Nemeroff and Rozin, "The Makings of the Magical Mind," 3. Italics removed.

negative. When negative, terms including "contamination" or "pollution" are often applied. Typically, negative valences are more predominant than positive valences. This should not be surprising based on what we've learned from Douglas. The world is messy, and cracks and crevices are everywhere. Opportunities for negative valences resulting from contact or association with something that doesn't perfectly fit a category seems more likely than instances of perfect matches.

The phrase "you are what you eat" is illustrative of contagious magical thinking. Contagious magical thinking holds that the properties of one object will be transferred to another upon contact. Nemeroff and Rozin looked for evidence of contagious magical thinking among American undergraduates by creating scenarios of two fictitious cultures. Embedded in each account was information about foods typically eaten by members of each culture. When students were asked to re-describe these cultures, the communities were described as exhibiting characteristics of the food consumed. Boar eaters were rated as more boar-like than those who did not consume boar.[27] The magical essence of the boar was viewed, however vaguely, as being transferred to the consumer. Notions of contagion are also at work in the aversion that many people express at the prospect of wearing a sweater worn by a serial killer. The most pressing anxiety concerns the intuition that somehow the tainted essence of the killer will wear off on anyone else who puts on the sweater.

In sympathetic magical thinking, the transfer of essence from one thing to another (contagion) establishes a continuing connection between the target and the source. With both similarity and contagion, some sort of efficacious "stuff" is posited as a key aspect of its identity, whatever it happens to be. How this essence is imagined varies. In Nemeroff and Rorzin's findings, for some, this essence is consistently imagined as a physical residue. For others, some sort of invisible spiritual essence is posited. More often than not, the imagining isn't exact. Magical thinkers can be pretty vague about the contours of sympathy.[28]

---

27. Nemeroff and Rozin, "The Makings of the Magical Mind," 8–9.
28. Nemeroff and Rozin, "The Makings of the Magical Mind," 16–17.

Nemeroff and Rozen conclude their observations with the comment that "magical thinking is an important part of human life, yet it has been little studied and hence is poorly understood."[29] In the way that our primer on evil has been set up here, magical thinking is an important part of making classification systems palpable. Magical thinking contributes a degree of veridicality to classification, a higher degree of realism. Competing classification systems are draped on our bodies, physical and social. As this happens, each part of the body is assigned an essence upon which one or another classification system hangs.[30] As a system, the ensemble appears to hold together, even though this shared world of names and expectations is imagined. Still, the emperor has never looked so good.

What I am proposing here is consistent with the observations of Nemeroff and Rozin, but I take their theory of magical thinking beyond their experimental definition. Using their suggestions as a starting point, perhaps less as laws and more as guiding norms, we can begin to map the scope and variances of dangers and aversions with an initial reference to dirt. Of particular interest is dirt that takes on magical properties through (perceived) offences or transgressions. As a first step in rethinking evil as dangers and aversions, we'll be looking at three examples: funerals in rural Cantonese society, social anxieties concerning drinking from the same cup during the ritual of Communion, and pollution anxieties in the novel *Dracula*.

Example 1: Death Pollution

Ah-bak [honorific uncle], who are those scruffy outsiders?
    Not so loud. Don't speak to them and don't go near them. They are [voice in a whisper] *ng jong lo*. They always come with the coffin. Such

---

29. Nemeroff and Rozin, "The Makings of the Magical Mind," 29.

30. For an excellent collection of essays addressing identity and body parts, see Howard Eilberg-Schwartz and Wendy Doniger, eds., *Off With Her Head! The Denial of Women's Identity in Myth, Religion, and Culture* (Berkeley, CA: University of California Press, 1995).

men are bad luck and their touch is very filthy.
—Elder of the Man lineage to J. L. W. during a funeral
in the village of San Tin, 1969.[31]

James and Rubie Watson conducted fieldwork in two rural villages in San Tin and Ha Tsuen, Hong Kong New Territories between 1969–1970 and 1977–1978. James Watson's account of death pollution illustrates the role magical thinking plays in fostering a wide set of dangers and aversions. The history and context of these dangers and aversions will be set aside as I cast a spotlight on the social dimensions of death pollution as interpreted by Watson. I do not cite the example because it exemplifies attitudes toward death pollution in other places. It does not. Instead, it is one of three examples to be discussed that illustrate and introduce diversity in our imagining of pollution, precautions, and purifications. When thinking about evil as dangers and aversions, it will be helpful to have a catalogue of their social dynamics—how they are imagined, and how they are remedied.

James Watson depicts the village rituals as being infused with a profound sense of fear and apprehension, as well as a profound desire to work through the perils of death pollution in order to facilitate the transformation of a dangerous corpse into a settled ancestor.[32] In the widest sense, funeral rituals obligate participants to take on a portion of death pollution as "the first transaction in a relationship of exchange between the living and the dead that stretches over many generations."[33] Participation in rituals of death and mourning are highly gendered, with women taking on vast majority of the

---

31. James L. Watson, "Funeral Specialists in Cantonese Society: Pollution, Performance, and Social Hierarchy," in James L. Watson and Rubie S. Watson, *Village Life in Hong Kong: Politics, Gender, and Ritual in the New Territories* (Hong Kong: Chinese University Press, 2004), 391.

32. Much of the following is taken from James L. Watson, "Of Flesh and Bones: The Management of Death Pollution in Cantonese Society" and "Funeral Specialists in Cantonese Society: Pollution, Performance, and Social Hierarchy" in *Village Life in Hong Kong: Politics, Gender, and Ritual in the New Territories* (Hong Kong: Chinese University Press, 2004).

33. Watson, "Of Flesh and Bones," 356.

dangerous ritual labor—a point to which we will return at the end of this section.[34]

There are two aspects of pollution that concern the villagers: the release of the spirit from the corpse and the "killing airs" (*saat hei*) released by the decaying flesh. Although the villagers make no such distinction, there is an implicit sense that the spirit, which can easily become confused or unsettled, presents an active danger to the living. Killing airs, on the other hand, are present in a more passive sense, affecting everyone equally.[35] They are thought to be released from the corpse at the moment of death, much "like an invisible cloud," and contaminate everything within the vicinity.[36] Contamination may bring misfortune and illness and is especially dangerous to pregnant women, newborn children, and young animals. During the funeral procession, ancestral tablets and images of deities are shielded, small shrines are screened, and windows and doors closed.[37] Active death pollution is not linguistically marked by the villagers but is discernable by noticing "points of aversion," the practice of looking away at moments when the spirit of the deceased may become agitated.

Given that death pollution produced by decaying flesh is imagined as a kind of miasma, there is a wide range of prophylactic rituals and precautions taken by ritual experts and mourners. Patches of red cloth may be attached to clothing to protect against and neutralize the killing airs of death pollution.[38] The priests also use ritual objects to mediate contact with the coffin (scissors wrapped in red yarn, for example).[39] Piping, wailing, and chanting are means of placating and calming the spirit of the deceased. While some of the killing airs can be absorbed by ritual items, such as coins or money used as payment for professionals (priest, corpse handlers, piper), part of the ceremony requires that some of the death pollution be absorbed into the

---

34. Watson notes male participation seems to center around the theme of property inheritance while female participation seems to focus on the theme of fertility.

35. Watson, "Of Flesh and Bones," 360.

36. Watson, "Of Flesh and Bones," 359.

37. Watson, "Of Flesh and Bones," 368.

38. Watson, "Of Flesh and Bones," 369.

39. Watson, "Funeral Specialists in Cantonese Society," 400.

flesh of the living. Almost everyone involved in the funeral ritual participates in the absorption of death pollution, no one more so than the eldest son. Despite the crucial role of the eldest son, women disproportionately attend funerals. Understanding why this is the case will give us clues as to how gender coding is intimately related to dangers and aversions and how they are dealt with.

Women interviewed by Watson suggest that their disproportionate participation at funerals is in large part because the men are too busy.[40] Watson presents his own ideas about this and suggests it has more to do with gender coding (*yang* is associated with masculinity and bones and *yin* is associated with femininity and flesh). Men participate in death rituals in accord with their obligations regarding the inheritance of property, especially the bones of the deceased and the estate. In this way, man's essence as *yang* is reproduced in perpetuity. Women participate in the death ritual in accord with conceptions of fertility. Despite the dangers of death pollution, married daughters and daughters-in-law rub their hair against the coffin, carrying pieces of green cloth symbolizing fertility (as opposed to the prophylactic red which neutralizes death pollution). Watson speculates that, by absorbing death pollution, the villagers take death into the realm of the living in order to produce life. Women's *yin* essence reproduces the fleshy and thus more temporal aspects of life.

The social forms that are produced and reproduced by funerals are telling. Watson observes that norms of death pollution reflect and maintain an existing division between the roles of women and men. They also create a social hierarchy. The closer one is to the source of the pollution—the decaying flesh of the corpse—the more polluted the target. Relations with those perceived as polluted are curtailed. Corpse handlers are viewed as the most polluted. Women participate in death rituals far more saliently than men. Their supposed essence as women is tied to this participation, which establishes their place within the community as much as it reflects it.

Although I am identifying evil through the framework of dangers and aversions, it is important to remember to avoid bringing our moralistic prejudices alongside this definition. Dangers and aversions are

---

40. Watson, "Of Flesh and Bones," 363.

not clear-cut. Not everything that is dangerous is "bad." Watson very keenly illustrates this in his observation that young married women rub their hair against the coffin. The polluting power of the killing airs has a life-giving dynamic as well. They may be dangerous for men as individuals, but they are dangerous and efficacious for female fertility and altogether necessary for ancestors and descendants alike.[41]

We should also note that how women and men understand death pollution in these villages may be different. While women's association with fertility and flesh helps explain their non-existence in the ancestral realm from the male point of view, there is undoubtedly an alternative view from the women in the village. This is discernable through the gaps and omissions of Watson's account. Women are responsible for mourning and lamentation, which may have its own cultural and social dynamic that men are unaware of. Women are also unofficial funeral experts.[42] Watson speculates that their expertise is self-taught but, as Rubie Watson notes, "affinal networks" of women have been known to be a source of security and identity.[43]

We can easily see how sympathetic magical thinking or something closely resembling this dynamic is at work. Upon death, a dangerous and contagious miasma is released. Rituals and symbols may protect and neutralize the dangers of killing airs but some of this dangerous essence must be absorbed by the living. According to Watson's reports, the male villagers have strong ideas about death pollution but are not especially precise about the details. We can describe this as an expression of magical thinking—a mode of thinking about things that posits a non-obvious essence, ripe with a range of dangers and aversions. Precision is not key here, nor is universal agreement. Even with a surface reading, we see that village women and male professionals have differing views about how this pollution works. Everyone would appear to agree that death pollution is present, but it is simultaneously vague enough to be subject to conflicting interpretation and durable enough to be reproduced over time.

---

41. Watson, "Of Flesh and Bones," 363.

42. Watson, "Funeral Specialists in Cantonese Society," 397–399.

43. Rubie Watson, "Class Differences and Affinal Relations in South China," *Village Life in Hong Kong*, 98. Affinal relations are relations established by marriage.

I will stress here that we should avoid thinking of the principles of magical thinking as laws in any literal sense. They help us adjust our sights, but we should be prepared to see that the contingencies of social life rarely conform to the theory, however sophisticated the theory. A theory of magical thinking brings into focus our capacity for imaginatively imbuing material things with essences. When we do this, we also create social hierarchies, boundaries, and ritual obligations—a system, or at least the illusion of a system.[44]

Example 2: Impurity and the Cup

Daniel Sack observes that, prior to the advent of germ theory in the 1870s, many Protestant Christians in the United States routinely drank wine from a common cup as part of the ritual of Eucharist (a ceremony of commemoration typically including bread and wine). This practice of sharing a single cup was eventually challenged as part of a larger sanitation crusade. While it might be said that germ theory instigated this crusade against impurity, the explanations given by critics of the shared cup show a tight-knit association of "whitebread" cleanliness, godliness, and gentility. As Sack notes, the objections arising from critics have more to do with the boundaries of the church and the "fear of contamination by other worshippers at the Communion rail" than with the dangers of bacteria.[45]

Sack begins this discussion with a brief overview of the abolition movement in the United States. He notes that the question of menu—of what should be served at the Communion rail—dovetailed with a question of method. How should Christians take their wine (or grape juice): a single shared cup or each their own individual cup?

---

44. Bloch, *In and Out of Each Other's Bodies*, 28–29.

45. The difficulty here, of course, is that bacteria can be spread through contact. This fact should not lead us to miss the point. Cleanliness, godliness, and gentility were all threatened with possible contamination. Even if bacteria can be spread from a shared cup, that's not how the objection ran or how the issue was imagined. Bacteria was used as a symbol that included a negative association with a wide range of associations including health, heredity, ethnicity, race, and religion.

The question is telling because it speaks to another kind of perceived danger and aversion: contamination from one's neighbors. While medical professionals developed and promoted germ theory in the 1870s, many laypeople across Protestant denominations came to suspect the practice of sharing the Communion cup of being more than just unhygienic. The shared Communion cup rapidly became a register of a wide range of social anxieties about contact with others, especially those outside one's social class. Sanitation crusades lead by white Protestants began to associate perceived lapses of hygiene with an ever-increasing scope of events in American life: alcohol, bad diet, gambling, immigration, crime, prostitution, smoking, urbanization, and so on.[46] These reform movements aim to remake the world in accord with an emergent and newly idealized image of white middle-class Protestants—"clean, safe, and orderly."[47] This fantasy of purity and order, Protestants concluded, was threatened by the upheavals of the late 1800s.

Sack writes, "The sanitation obsession of the Protestant middle class reflects worries about the broad changes in American society. By controlling disease, white Protestants hoped to control a society slipping out of their grasp." Sack suggests that "there was more involved than just fear of contagion." In the battle against disease, "cleanliness was not just next to godliness, in many cases it *was* godliness."[48] Clean bodies came to be associated with moral purity, and this conceit led to anxieties about "sharing a Communion cup with strangers—particularly the poor and other social outcasts."[49] Proper hygiene, as defined by medical experts, was tantamount to proper Christianity.

In 1887 M. O. Terry, a doctor in Utica, New York, expressed concern that an open invitation to share the Communion cup would lead to some sort of dangerous contamination: "The old lady, pure in mind and body, sips from the cup which has just left the lips of

---

46. Daniel Sack, "Purity and the Cup," *Whitebread Protestants* (New York: Palgrave, 2000), 32–34.

47. Sack, "Purity and the Cup," 33. This image of safety, of course, means safety for some and not others.

48. Sack, "Purity and the Cup," 34.

49. Sack, "Purity and the Cup," 35.

one physically impure ... [while] the old lady's pure and healthy child takes the cup from the unfortunate child of heredity, the offspring of physical impurity."[50] Laypeople criticized clergy for participating in rituals that belonged to a "primitive age" and an "impure past," soaked in traditions of "cruel fanaticism, bigotry, ignorance and superstition."[51] The shared cup was deemed a "menace to public health," and single cup advocates freely reinterpreted the past practices of Jesus and his disciplines to conform to the "good manner, healthfulness, decency and convenience" purported by the middle-class reform movements.[52] Jesus was imagined to drink unfermented non-alcoholic wine served in individual cups. Despite the presence of the diseased, the sick, and the afflicted, "Christ [was] fitly represented. No sin-afflicted one could say that he was tempted or his appetite for drink aroused. No one with the glow of health could be tainted. The bread and the cup, like Christ, were pure, free and life-giving."[53] The innovation was apparently so inspiring to some clergy that a few suggested that "individual cups might put an end to the necessity of separate congregations for the whites and colored throughout the South"—a comment that prompted James Buckley, editor of the *Christian Advocate* to write "The superficiality of this remark probably accounts for its brutality."[54]

---

50. Terry quoted in Sack, "Purity and the Cup," 36.

51. Howard Anders quoted in Sack, "Purity and the Cup," 38.

52. Sack, "Purity and the Cup," 39.

53. WCTU member cited in Sack, "Purity and the Cup," 47.

54. Buckley, quoted in Sack, "Purity and the Cup," 43. James Buckley, editor the *Christian Advocate* (a weekly newspaper of the Methodist Episcopal Church). To provide a bit of context, Buckley notes that some clergy were supportive of moving to individual cups. Individual cups may eliminate segregation since there would be no contact through the use of a shared cup and this would create a stronger sense of community. That segregation was cast as required because of the Communion cup lead Buckley to make the comment "The superficiality of this remark probably accounts for its brutality" (43). Buckley, defender of church authority and tradition, further noted that the individual cup would in fact move in the opposite direction and would sponsor "the formation of caste churches, the freezing out of such as were disagreeable" (43).

Clerical critics of the reform movement were not in short supply. For some, the whole issue suggested that we surrender the soul to the body. A Lutheran pastor concerned about the influence of the devil in history wondered, "if the seemingly innocent use of grape juice and individual glasses is not just one more extension of this satanic manipulation?"[55] Despite pushback from clergy and despite the liturgical reform movements in the 1960s, the individual cup largely won out. The debate was renewed in the US in the early 1980s with the AIDS epidemic, and advocates on both sides weighed in.

Magical thinking is clearly at work in perceptions of the shared cup. While germ theory emphasizes the transmission of physical substances through contact, the concern of reform-minded Protestants was not limited to germs. Their imagining of some transfer of essences, never defined in particular, plays on racist and classist anxieties about contact with others. Whether based on disease, heredity, race, or the disordered soul of the unhygienic, white Protestants came to feel their (imagined) purity threatened by even the slightest contact with others. Consequently, they created new physical accommodations for the ritual in question, thus reinterpreting the ritual and their own history as they shifted the practice.

While germ theory coupled with a microscope pinpointed a precise cause of transmission, the reform movement had no such limitations. Impurity presumedly resulted from physical contact, one person to another. Anxiety appears to be in close proportion to the heightened classism and individualism of the Protestants discussed in Sack's book, most of whom taught a gospel of "personal responsibility, private morality, and social gentility."[56] The perceived dangers of contamination from the shared cup ranged from risking sickness and disease to wholesale spiritual malady and ungodliness. The aversion to sharing a drink with one's neighbors had a profound effect on the meaning and practice of Communion in many Protestant churches. Is Communion a re-enactment of the Passover Seder with Jesus or simply a tradition reflecting continuity? Is Communion a mystical

---

55. Cited in Sack, "Purity and the Cup," 49.
56. Sack, "Purity and the Cup," 33.

experience for each individual worshipper or a symbol of communal experience of all participants?[57]

The emphasis on dangers and aversions once again draws us into patterns of interaction where people are ranked and included or excluded on the basis of classification. That these ranking systems make reference to invisible essences is notable, especially when these imagined essences are able to transform the identity and status of someone by means of contact or, in some instances, simple symbolic association. In the case of Cantonese funerals, death pollution is perceived to emanate from the decaying flesh of the corpse. It clings to the places, objects, and people it comes into contact with. This passive invisible essence is highly contagious and can only be resisted by ritual means. Perhaps guided by intuitive forms of cognition, magical thinking services a myriad of social formations: property inheritance, feminine fertility, the ritual authority of specialists, and so on. In the case of the cup, transmission is imagined as shared (magical) contact with a drinking vessel. Magical thinking is present in both, but how the dangers and aversions work is a function of a particular context.

Example 3: The Abomination

Bram Stoker's *Dracula* has become one of my favorite novels. The word "Dracula" alone has become synonymous with evil and inhumanity. In many respects, my ongoing reflections on this novel opened the door to this volume, so it seems fitting to work it into the first chapter focused on key categories. The essay "The Blood is the Life" by Timothy Beal draws explicitly on Douglas's *Purity and Danger* to make the point that *Dracula* "is a story of English ritual purity and danger."[58] Throughout the essay, Beal draws our attention to the myriad ways in which Dracula threatens the established categories of "good English." When I use the novel in my course Evil in World Religions, the final assignment requires that students read the novel not as a novel but

---

57. Sack, "Purity and the Cup," 59.

58. Timothy Beal, "The Blood is the Life," *Religion and Its Monsters* (New York: Routledge, 2001), 124.

as a collection of papers found in an archive. My students draw on the required readings to provide an explanation as to why Dracula was hunted and killed and why the people discussed in the documents refused to contact the proper authorities in doing so.

In the context of the novel, the characters' actions make sense. Dracula is a demon, an incarnation of supernatural evil. But if we treat the novel as a set of archival documents, we have a bit of a mystery. What prompted the good fellowship of the light to see the Count as a cosmic impurity that must be obliterated and not simply called to court? Why did those described in these documents decide to annihilate Dracula instead of ask for an account of his actions? In a curious way, this volume is designed to answer that question. How and when do we create monsters? And when we create these figures of abomination, how do they end up beyond the pale of consideration and destined to be annihilated without a word?

As Beal correctly observes, *Dracula* is a novel of purity and danger. The Count is an exemplary figure of inversion and contradiction, because of his intimate connection to chaos. He embodies the uncanny at every turn, familiar and strange: cultured, but not in English culture; reasoning, but more cunning than deliberative; living, but dead. It isn't that Dracula escapes classification. He doesn't—Dracula is an abomination. However, he's classified as an abomination, a creature of impurity, because of a perceived connection to dirt as matter out of place—evidenced by how he twists and contorts familiar categories. Dracula is a veritable potpourri of images and associations designed to pull the reader in several directions at once. His namesake makes reference to the devils and dragons of the Apocalypse of John. His powers prompted Jonathan Harker to exclaim, "What manner of man is this?," referencing a passage from Matthew. Like Jesus as described in the canonical Gospels, Dracula also commands the weather.[59]

The abomination of Dracula comes into full focus in the "primal scene," which includes the assault of Mina Harker. The scene takes place after Jonathan Harker's imprisonment and return from Dracula's castle, as well as Lucy Westenra's death and subsequent

---

59. Beal, "The Blood is the Life," 125.

necrotic rebirth (and destruction) as a vampire at the hands (or fangs) of Dracula. Beal writes:

> The scene is a mix of maternal intimacy, sexual violence, and adultery. Jonathan lay dazed on the bed, "his face flush and breathing heavily as though in a stupor," while Mina knelt beside him being force-nursed from Dracula's bosom: "his right hand gripped her by the back of the neck, forcing her face down on his bosom. Her white nightdress was smeared with blood, and a thin stream trickled down the man's bare breast, which was shown by the torn-open dress."[60]

Beal draws on the biblical allusions to register the abominations of Dracula: the illicit consumption of blood, the undermining of patriarchal possession, the contamination of marital union, and the blurring of maternal and paternal roles.[61] These violations draw the reader into a world where "the old centuries had, and have powers of their own which mere 'modernity' cannot kill."[62] By prompting us to enter into the world of the archaic, Dracula is uncoupled from the norms of the present and subject to a ritual instead of a moral or legal judgement. As a creature of impurity, Dracula must be cleansed (or made orderly), through what Beal calls "rituals of resacralization."[63]

In the novel, resacralization occurs in several instances. The first is the failed scientific attempt, the blood transfusions with Lucy. Van Helsing tries to purify Lucy's blood through the emerging technology of blood transfusion. The second attempt brings the reader into an archaic world of violence and impurity. After Lucy appears from her tomb in the form of a vampire, she is eventually forced back into the coffin where her living-dead body is mutilated. The starkness of this violence is contrasted with the "holy calm" of her lifeless corpse and her face of "unequalled sweetness and purity."[64] Lucy's contact with chaos transforms her into a creature of disorder. Only a ritual of purification returns her disordered state to the beautiful banality of

---

60. Beal, "The Blood is the Life," 132.

61. Beal, "The Blood is the Life," 132–133.

62. Jonathan Harker quoted in Beal, "The Blood is the Life," 127. This quote is misattributed to Abraham Van Helsing.

63. Beal, "The Blood is the Life," 134–140.

64. Beal, "The Blood is the Life," 137.

order. As Beal puts it, the destruction of Dracula is a "reenactment of a mythic chaos battle."[65] He is chased back to his homeland and executed under the golden light of the setting sun. Dracula's destruction marks the final resacralization of the novel. The surviving men kneel in earnest "Amen," and Mina notes that with the disappearance of her mark of uncleanness "The curse has passed away!"[66]

The two forms of magical thinking, similarity and contagion, are useful and provocative lenses for interpreting the novel. The novel *Dracula* presents us with a wide collection of threats and contagions, not simply reducible to the exchange of blood. Much of the novel is situated by the possibility of recuperating purity after contamination, and it becomes possible to speak of impurity in terms of ritual impurity. Ritual purification can then be viewed as a creative way in which communities deal with the contingencies of contagion and its dangers. It may help us understand the violence of purification. Even in a work of fiction, we can see that when we focus on the taint of corruption, there may be a tendency to neglect the humanity of those involved.

Conclusion

Classification and sympathetic magical thinking play an important role in many of our assessments of dangers and aversions. If Douglas is correct, anxieties about impurity and contagion are unavoidable aspects of everyday life. Life is messy and contradictory. In the context of magical thinking, all of this mess makes it easy and almost intuitive to point to an outside power interfering with orderly existence. In each of the examples above, we have seen how the perceived instabilities of life contribute to an interest in the classification, re-classification, and containment of dangerous contagious essences and events. In each instance, these dangers are tied to larger patterns of social interaction than Nemeroff and Rozin's theory of sympathetic magical thinking can begin to account for. While there is an imagined

---

65. Beal, "The Blood is the Life," 138.
66. Quoted in Beal, "The Blood is the Life," 139.

efficacious essence to death pollution, an imagined impurity in sharing cups, or a demonic spirit in Dracula's undead flesh, each of these dangers is taken up into a wider network of social arrangements and arranging. Property relations, kinship, gender roles and hierarchies are all implicated in these perceived dangers and aversions.

The key categories and illustrations here serve as an initial step in considering evil as a critical concept. Human beings are classificatory creatures. We organize our environments in ways we find meaningful and, in doing so, create spaces of danger and aversion. Because many of these dangers accrue within the cracks and contradictions of our categories, people as a matter of course create procedures and protocols for dealing with anomalies and ambiguities. Our categories may reflect a larger cosmological worldview of good and evil, or they may fit together in a series of overlapping status functions reflecting a division of labor. Many of these anxiety-producing events are dealt with by means of ritual. Gender asymmetries coalesce around death pollution and create unofficial cultures of female ritual expertise. Classism, racism, and homophobia are reproduced at the Communion rail in the name of science. In the example of Dracula, we see how the segregation of people based on attributed essences results in a determination to destroy offenders at all costs, overriding or uncoupling any moral sensibilities. In each case, we see both classification and magical thinking at work. However, we also see ritual and ritualization as a means of dealing with border skirmishes and contradictions, so it is to ritual that we turn next.

Chapter 3

Ritual and Authority

In class I often start the lecture on anthropologist Maurice Bloch's work by featuring a series of images collected from various keyword searches I've done over the years.[1] I ask students about the images and whether the people represented in the images appear to be part of some sort of ritual. I also ask why they think this is the case. Without any substantial background in ritual theory, many of the students select aspects of the images they think are suggestive of ritual activity. Some of these selections include the separation of women and men, the color coding of clothing, the style of clothing worn, the bodily comportment of people featured in the images, the presence of iconographic representations, and so on. Unsurprisingly, students pick up on a large variety of possible cues. Human beings are highly adept at noticing and identifying all kinds of non-linguistic forms of communication such as posture, expression, and colorful signaling. We often notice small details, gestures, and variances. We read bodies like we read written works.[2] Importantly, we encounter and

---

1. The eclectic collection includes images of people engaged in daily routines (drinking coffee), funerals, sporting events, birthday celebrations, worship, practicing yoga, singing in a choir, and a graduation ceremony. Some of the keywords used include targeted searches such as "public rituals" and "birthday parties" while others were vague, including "traditions" and "holidays."

2. This is a point that comes up again and again in most of the ethnographic literature. Without coming up with an extensive list, I'll simply refer to Pentecostal attention to healthy and unhealthy bodies discussed in Kate Bowler, *Blessed* (Oxford: Oxford University Press, 2013), the way in which Baptists read the rhetoric and bodies of their preachers, discussed in Susan F. Harding, *The Book of Jerry Falwell* (Princeton, NJ: Princeton University Press, 2000), and the rules and guidelines for bodily comportment referenced in Carol Delaney, *The Seed and Soil: Gender and Cosmology in Turkish Village Society* (Berkeley, CA: University of California

pay attention to the details of our environment from within our conditioned frames of reference. This contextualized attention to detail is an entry point into understanding other cultures and communicative expressions as much as it may lead to misunderstandings. Robin Wall Kimmerer's discussion of her frustration with middle-aged vision (and the need for reading glasses) lead her to recall a poignant example from her travels:

> My fruitless strain to see what I know is right in front of me reminds me of my first trip into the Amazon rain forest. Our indigenous guides would patiently point out the iguana resting on a branch or the toucan looking down at us through the leaves. What was so obvious to their practiced eyes was nearly invisible to us. Without practice, we simply couldn't interpret the pattern of light and shadow as "iguana" and so it remained right before our eyes, frustratingly unseen.[3]

While I am not convinced by Robert McCauley and Thomas Lawson's theory of ritual competence, which suggests human beings have the intuitive capacity to recognize ritual actions, I do think we notice nuances like differing styles or modes of presentation and the coordination of action.[4] What we notice about human behavior, however, is related to what we've learned to notice. There is a close relation between ritual and expertise, just as there is ritual and authority.

Of all the accounts of ritual and ritualization I've come across, Maurice Bloch's is the most compelling.[5] Bloch conceives of ritual as a mode of human organization that structures action by means

---

Press, 1991). For a compelling study of how we perceive even slight inflections in speech, see Harris, *Trusting What You're Told*.

3. For the importance of cueing and memory, see D. M. Oppenheimer, "The Secret Life of Fluency," *Trends in Cognitive Sciences* 12 (2008), 237–241; Robin Wall Kimmerer, *Gathering Moss: A Natural and Cultural History of Mosses* (Corvallis, OR: Oregon State University Press, 2003), 7.

4. E. Thomas Lawson and Robert N. McCauley, *Rethinking Religion: Connecting Cognition and Culture* (Cambridge: Cambridge University Press, 1993).

5. Maurice Bloch, "Symbols, Song, Dance and Features of Articulation: Is Religion an Extreme Form of Traditional Authority?," *European Journal of Sociology/Archives Européennes de Sociologie* 15, no. 1 (1974), 55–81.

of reduction and limitation. In his view, the main features of rituals are predictability and authority. Ritualization refers to contexts of authority or authorization that prescribe or compel sequential action such that the performers surrender creative options and orient their responses in a single direction. Ritual contexts are moments when human activity can be anticipated in advance because of the implicit or explicit strictures placed on communication.

In "Symbols, Song, Dance and Features of Articulation," Bloch challenges the assumptions of anthropologists and scholars of religion who interpret symbols and symbolic features of rituals as everyday instances of communication. He maintains that symbols should not be treated as ordinary linguistic units, filled with meaning and possibility, but as something much more peculiar. Instead of asking about meaning, Bloch starts with a different question: How does ritual make its statements appear powerful and holy?[6] He argues that only when we recognize the distinctive features of ritualized communication will we have a better understanding of the power of formalized ritual and its rather uncanny relation to ordinary language.[7]

While Bloch is asking how ritual makes statements appear holy, most important for our purposes here is how rituals relate to dangers and aversions and how rituals contribute to the enrichment and emboldening of categories. While repetition is often an obvious feature of ritual action, the more interesting feature, for Bloch, is

---

6. Bloch, "Symbols, Song, Dance," 57.

7. Although belonging to a different theoretical framework, Habermas's distinction between instrumental and communicative action and between locutionary, illocutionary, and perlocutionary speech acts offers us another way of describing this. Communicative action aims at mutual understanding and agreement. Instrumental action aims at success. To re-describe Bloch in Habermasian terms, formalization transforms illocutionary and locutionary aspects of communicative action into perlocutionary affects of instrumental action. Habermas, *The Theory of Communicative Action*, trans. Thomas McCarthy (Boston, MA: Beacon Press, 1984), vol. 1, 273–337. The impoverishing of language that Bloch speaks of is the result of the steering mechanic of instrumental action. This re-description of Bloch addresses some of the upstream concerns briefly raised by Caroline Humphrey and James Laidlaw, *The Archetypal Actions of Ritual* (Oxford: Oxford University Press, 1994), 84–85.

compulsion. On the occasions that rituals must be performed, they must be performed *properly*. The more formalized the occasion, the more compulsory the action and the more dangerous deviance becomes. But even in informal situations, there are still very specific expectations. In my experience, the modern birthday celebration is a fairly informal event, but there are rules. Invited guests don't open the birthday presents, although they can help if asked. If there is a birthday cake, the expectation is that it will be presented to the guests whole, without pieces missing. A birthday gift can embarrass but should not shame the recipient. These snippets of etiquette are all in place to ensure a successful birthday ritual. Deviance is to be avoided and may even qualify as dangerous, especially if perceived to be a threat to the social fabric.

Bloch begins his essay by observing that the language used in ritual is distinct from ordinary use of language. Rituals often contain fixed or highly stylized features such as song and dance. With reference to his research on the Merina circumcision ceremony, he notes that the language in the ritual includes formal oratory (speaking the words of the ancestors), intoning (chanting), and sequential singing.[8] Unlike the spontaneity of ordinary communication, language in ritual is marked by its unusual form. Ritualized language tends to be less flexible and more fixated on particular iterations. Oratory may draw on a limited set of sources, chanting may involve only modest variation in tone and cadence, and songs may be performed with exacting precision over and over again.

Rituals are characterized by their relative predictability as well as their capacity to solicit or cajole obedience. Acquiescence is often achieved by means of sequencing or coding, the use of scripts that regulate acceptable behavior. Rituals are often orchestrated and are expected to be performed with relative accuracy. This means that the formal elements within a ritual or ritualized context limit our communicative options: "Ritual is an occasion where syntactic and other linguistic freedoms are reduced."[9] More than this, rituals have a tempting or captivating character. Bloch notes, "the ceremonial

---

8. Bloch, "Symbols, Song, Dance," 58–59.
9. Bloch, "Symbols, Song, Dance," 56.

trappings of a highly formalized situation seem to *catch* the actors so that they are unable to resist the demands made on them."[10] He calls this distinctive feature *formal*, and the process of shaping language into ritual a process of *formalization*. Formalization catches us in the act and can be described as an impoverished or highly curtailed use of language, a stylized interaction wherein interpretive options at all levels of language are abandoned.[11] For example, formal oratories rely on a set of stock phrases, intoning has a fixed cadence, and songs are looped and repeated without alteration. To press the arthritic quality of formalized language, Bloch suggests the sentence "The cat sat on the mat" can be formulated in eighty-one possible sentences based on variations in tense, intonation, and nouns. With one restriction on intonation, this shifts from eighty-one to twenty-seven possible iterations. With two restrictions from eighty-one to three. With a relatively small number of stipulations, linguistic options can be almost completely eliminated.[12]

In contrasting ordinary speech with formalized speech, Bloch argues that, in formalized speech, "the ability of language to communicate messages concerning particular events and its ability to convey specific messages leading to particular action disappears."[13] Formalized language is restricted by stipulations, traditions, or codes. These restrictions also inhibit semantic potential and creativity. These limitations curb what we can say and how we can say it, thereby reducing our capacity for specificity and accuracy in describing the world around us. Formalized language, in this view, becomes not only increasingly predictable but also sequentially uncoupled from ordinary people, places, and events.[14] This is why Bloch argues that formalization results in what we can call traditional or

---

10. Bloch, "Symbols, Song, Dance," 59–60.
11. Bloch, "Symbols, Song, Dance," 60.
12. Bloch, "Symbols, Song, Dance," 61.
13. Bloch, "Symbols, Song, Dance," 62.
14. Bloch, "Symbols, Song, Dance," 62. In class I ask my students to describe what it means to take a course on the study of religion at a university with the following restrictions: you cannot mention anything to do with teaching or learning. As Bloch notes, when you "interpret" symbols that are primarily performative in nature and in context, what you end up with is a lot of gobbledygook (75).

religious authority. Taking the example of formal oratory, a speaker may be restricted in terms of the kinds of texts that can be cited. An American evangelical pastor may, by the authority of tradition, limit their citations in a sermon to passages from the Bible, the words of other male pastors, and testimony from the congregation. Because of the close relation between masculinity and authority, citing a male football coach or male sports celebrity may also be acceptable.

To be sure, some degree of formalization exists in all our relationships. Limits to communicative freedom may side with respectful and mutual encouragement or be indications of customary forms of etiquette. In a formal hierarchy, when an authority figure addresses someone in a lower position with a request, the latter often does not have the capacity to say no or dissent. In these contexts, speakers or ritual performers are able to work coercively in what Bloch refers to as a form of social control.[15] Going back to a previous example, the Cantonese funeral priest who may otherwise be thought of as a charlatan by the villagers is able to command the terrified funeral participants into precise and absolutely necessary action—even with physical force if necessary.[16] In highly formalized settings, the proper performance of a sequence is simply viewed as necessary.

The implications of this kind of stylized communication should not be underestimated. The reduced capacity of language to refer to and abstract from a particular context makes every reference seem to point back to the same thing. Specificity evaporates into repetition, and repetition makes all events appear the same.[17] This sameness creates an illusion of transcendence. As disparate occurrences are merged in this way, their temporal index disappears and their presence as eternal or otherworldly moves into the foreground. Formalized presentations appear ahistorical because they are not organized in the same way as ordinary language. It isn't that rituals are separate from everything else. Due to the restrictions and limitations of their form, rituals create a cloistered sphere of impoverished language that feels separate or uncoupled from ordinary

15. Bloch, "Symbols, Song, Dance," 63, 64.
16. Watson, "Funeral Specialists in Cantonese Society," 402–403.
17. Bloch, "Symbols, Song, Dance," 62.

reality because of the compelling power of authority and the perceived necessity of the sequential action. When skeptics of theories
of power ask what power feels like, I'm usually prompted to say "It
feels like a ritual." Formalization compels practice and establishes
non-compliance as dangerous.

The difference between formal and informal language can be captured as performative force versus propositional force. Performative
force results from a way of using language with the aim of influencing
by means of affect and restriction. Performative force has success
in reaching a goal as its motivating factor. Propositional force is the
language of questioning and criticism. Propositional force is conver-
sational, motivated by an interest in understanding something with
someone without restriction or the powers of affect.[18] In this sense,
traditional authority and ritual are quasi-discursive forms of communication, which is why Bloch suggests that a definition of religion as
an explanation or a speculation about our place in the world is mis-
guided: "Religion is the last place to find anything 'explained' because
as we have seen religious communication rules out the very tools of
explanation."[19] If we can imagine informal and formal language along
a spectrum, we have unrestricted speech on one side moving through
to higher levels of restriction. Higher levels of restriction denote traditional authority and, at, the far end of formalization, we have what
Bloch calls "extreme religious authority." Extreme religious authority
minimizes or eliminates propositional force. As Bloch puts it, "you
cannot argue with a song."[20] On the extreme side, the ordinary fluid-
ity of communication moves like molasses. Meaning is congealed as
words become mired in the context of a religious framework.[21] At this
point, words within a sphere of formalization "drift out of meaning"
since they cannot refer to any specific historical reality and can only
be repeated.[22] Answering the question posed at the beginning of his
study, Bloch observes that rituals appear holy, eternal, and powerful

---

18. Bloch, "Symbols, Song, Dance," 67.
19. Bloch, "Symbols, Song, Dance," 71.
20. Bloch, "Symbols, Song, Dance," 71.
21. Bloch, "Symbols, Song, Dance," 74.
22. Bloch, "Symbols, Song, Dance," 74.

because they have been protected from the contingencies of shifting contexts.

It is important to note that this vision of the eternal is an illusion created by the coercive effects of authority. Rituals are not uncoupled from history or politics. Rituals may create the feeling of being part of a great tradition, but this feeling is the affect of sequential coding, the compulsion of playing a prescribed role in a script. This is the fascinating power of ritual. Rituals must be performed and performed properly, but the words and symbols used within rituals are more like things that lack any possible capacity to explain or capture a piece of reality.[23] This is why Bloch suggests rituals should not be interpreted as sources of meaning. Instead, rituals are like "tunnels into which one plunges, and where, since there is no possibility of turning either to right or left, the only thing to do is to follow."[24] Their formalized characteristics prevent them from being full of meaning—at least within the ritual context. In ritual, reality is transformed into a timeless zone in which everything and everyone is in the right place. Immediate context transforms into eternal truth as history fades into repetition.[25] As Bloch suggests, "It is through the process of making a power situation appear a fact in the nature of the world that traditional authority works."[26]

Given their ahistorical façade, rituals are ambiguous and susceptible to manipulation, even if their formal qualities resist the kind of tinkering to which many social and political players aspire. The trafficking of ritual for social interests will be discussed more in the next chapter on myth and mythmaking. In the context of myth, rituals can be used to reproduce categories or put them in jeopardy. Rituals are opaque when it comes to meaning but also serve as (impoverished)

---

23. Bloch, "Symbols, Song, Dance," 75, 76. In a context that requires the coordination of action, meaning cannot be wholly eliminated. Symbols must contain at least some modicum of meaning to serve as vehicles of coordination. If the significance of a symbol has been completely lost, it will have to be supplemented with attending symbols (and thus given new significance at the same time).

24. Bloch, "Symbols, Song, Dance," 76.

25. Bloch, "Symbols, Song, Dance," 78.

26. Bloch, "Symbols, Song, Dance," 79.

vehicles for social coordination. Rituals can be used to maintain political power as much as they can be used to dissolve it.[27] In terms of dangers and aversions, rituals compel participation and compliance. Deviance can be viewed as a threat to the eternal order of things. According to the frame of this primer, disobedience within ritual could be a source of great evil.

We have seen that classification is an activity buttressed by magical thinking. Following Bloch, we can also see that worldviews and schemas are often formalized into systems of action and interaction. Highly formalized systems are lived out as rituals for eating, interacting with people, and laboring. Formalization creates bounded bodies in time and space, and those boundaries demarcate dangers and aversions, inside and out, friend and foe. In what follows, I will use three examples of formalization to show how rituals authorize and produce bounded space. The first—from Susan Harding's work on the power of witnessing within evangelical Christianity—is an example of how traditional authority is created. The second case study is an example of how rituals can be used to maintain traditional authority. For this, we turn to Heiko Henkel's account of an evening with friends in Turkey and the role of Muslim daily prayer. Finally, we examine how rituals can be used to challenge or dissolve authority. In this case study, we turn to the exhumation of corpses during a period of political unrest in Spain, as outlined by Bruce Lincoln.

Example 1: Witnessing

When working with Bloch's understanding of formalization, we must think outside the box of meaning. Often enough, we are asked to focus on the meaning of an event or text. We are expected to read or observe and interpret. Bloch's understanding of ritual, however, calls for a different approach. We assess the context in which symbols

---

27. An advantage of Bloch's approach is that it eschews any sharp distinction between religion and politics. Bloch, "Symbols, Song, Dance," 78, 79. As may be evident, the heuristic definition of religion provided in the Preface reflects what I take to be the insightful gains of Bloch's observations.

and language appear. Is the context formal or informal? If we fail to answer this question carefully, we risk a serious misunderstanding of the remarkable difference between performative power (language used to bring about a particular state of affairs) and propositional speech (language used to understand something with someone).

For example, if we take the statement "God exists" as a propositional statement, we might immediately rush toward definitions—the philosophy of religion, theology, and the catalogues of available evidence that could be cited to support such a claim. However, if we read this statement as part of a ritual and not as a propositional claim to be debated, we begin to see something quite different. If the statement "God exists" is part of a ritual sequence rather than a scientific proposition, it might help us understand the kind of frustrations expressed by "new atheist" Richard Dawkins in his book *The God Delusion*. Throughout this volume, Dawkins labors under the impression that theologians are committed to bad science because he's committed to the claim of God's existence as a scientific proposition. If that claim is seen as a ritual sequence, however, his protestations amount to an interruption of a theatrical performance midway. The ritual script demands the actor repeat their lines and so the lines are repeated.[28] Of course, we'll also head down the wrong path if we ignore the words being used. Bloch is careful to acknowledge that even the most extreme instances of formalization cannot be counted as absolutely devoid of meaning.

In this context, Susan Harding's essay on witnessing within fundamentalist evangelical Christianity serves as an excellent illustration of a process of formalization wherein a conversation is transformed into a ritual performance. Harding begins "Speaking is Believing" with an account of her departure from a meeting with Reverend Melvin Campbell at Jordan Baptist Church. She left the meeting in "some kind of daze," the aftermath of an intense witnessing session. While driving away from the encounter with Campbell, Harding was nearly hit by another vehicle and she immediately thought to herself,

---

28. Richard Dawkins in *The God Delusion* (Boston, MA: Houghton Mifflin, 2006).

"What is God trying to tell me?"[29] She goes on to observe, "It was my voice but not my language."[30]

Harding's essay about witnessing outlines how—by means of rhetorical technique, storied sequencing, and didactic performance—a speaker is able to situate, fracture, and reconstitute a listener, moving the listener through the sequence of unsaved to saved. While the ritual does not always result in conversion to born-again Christianity, it may vividly impress upon the listener the elemental features of a fundamentalist Baptist language. This language, Harding argues, comes to occupy or inhabit the listener.

In class I often ask my students when they've been possessed by language—when certain words and phrases bubble up into our heads and seem to block everything else out. We talk about clichés, commercial jingles, song lyrics, parental advice, and earworms. Most of us are familiar with how language possesses us and how difficult it can be to get a quickly annoying song out of your head. This is part of the power of formalization. It changes how we think, and it changes the words we use to think with. "Speaking is Believing" provides us with an excellent example of how formalization creates authority over a witting or unwitting participant:

> The process starts when an unsaved listener begins to appropriate in his or her inner speech the saved speaker's language and its attendant view of the world. The speaker's language, now in the listener's voice, converts the listener's mind into a contested terrain, a divided self. At the moment of salvation, which may come quickly and easily, or much later after great inward turmoil, the listener becomes a speaker. The Christian tongue locks into some kind of central, controlling, dominant place; it has gone beyond the point of inhabiting the listener's mind to occupy the listener's identity.[31]

Although witnessing has a dialogical or interactive structure, Harding argues that it "is no mere conversation" and is a ritual "shorn of

---

29. Harding, "Speaking is Believing," *The Book of Jerry Falwell: Fundamentalist Language and Politics*, 33.

30. Harding, "Speaking is Believing," 33.

31. Harding, "Speaking is Believing," 34.

almost all distraction."[32] Similar to Bloch's question about how rituals appear holy, Harding starts with the question: how does this ritual accomplish its aims? How does it quicken the supernatural imagination? How does it create an irrefutable reality?[33]

Harding's analysis identifies several formalized rhetorical techniques and outlines how these techniques appropriate a listener by assuming control over the dialogue.[34] While the ritual may have an informal semblance—just two people sitting down for a quiet conversation about serious things—its hypnotic features suggest something much more precise, practiced, and stylized. Harding identifies five rhetorical movements in this particular witnessing session:

> He equated his present listener—me—with the listeners in his stories. He fashioned her as lost. He fashioned the gospel speaker—himself and others—as saved. He transformed lost listeners in his stories into gospel speakers. And he invited me to undergo the same transformation, the same narrative rite of passage, and become a gospel speaker.[35]

Harding observes that witnessing speakers also employ a remarkably wide variety of rhetorical techniques. She indicates in her essay that it is difficult to convey the accent, cadence, intonation, pausing, pitch, and stress on the page. A more obvious technique appears with the rhetorical move that places the listener in the narrative and, in doing so, subjects the listener to "a whole range of presuppositions posited in such a way that they were difficult to resist."[36] Harding identifies verse markers ("and" and "now"), special codes, figurative language, symbolic and metaphoric parallelism, and appeals to tradition as part of the idiom of witnessing. The relation between the speaker and listener is also intensified by a particular use of pronouns: "I" and "you"

---

32. Harding, "Speaking is Believing," 37.

33. Harding, "Speaking is Believing," 36.

34. As these scripts are internalized, the listener also makes the script their own. Each transmission creates a new iteration.

35. Harding, "Speaking is Believing," 40.

36. Harding, "Speaking is Believing," 42.

and the co-optive "we."[37] As the ritual progresses, Harding contends that the listener is both enlisted and refashioned in the image created by the speaker.[38] At certain moments in the ritual, Campbell is able to solicit predictable and controlled responses from Harding:

> When a child is about to be born, it's first enclosed in the mother's womb. Is that true? [Yes.]
>
> Okay, Susan, you have the characteristics and traits of your mother and your father. True? ["Yes."][39]

Cadence, phrasing, laconic pace, and repetition all figure into Campbell's witnessing. The ritual may not compel a listener as larger more public rituals might, but the cadence of the ritual leaves "no space for inner speech." She describes her experience as being "caught" by Campbell's language.[40] Witnessing aims to reconstitute the self and transform that self into a new creation, but this new creation is a much more restricted self that is fashioned by the constraints and limitations of a fundamentalist rhetoric and cosmology.

What are the dangers here? Certainly the impetus behind the ritual is a concern for the soul of the listener. The evangelical regards the unsaved to be in mortal peril. That's one side of how formalization relates to dangers and aversions. But the other side concerns the consequences of dissent. Harding could have walked out. Her motives for staying are her own, but we can make some reasoned guesses. Harding's anthropological research involves interviewing fundamentalist preachers. In effect, she was at work, and, as a general rule, you don't leave work early. However, her intellectual interest in fundamentalist rhetoric may also have encouraged her to stay. She may have recognized that this particular interview, which turned into a witnessing session, may provide an excellent example of the power of rhetoric. But another reading is plausible, too: did Harding get caught in the ritual and simply feel that it had to be carried out until the

---

37. Harding, "Speaking is Believing," 42. I'm prone to using this technique myself, we're in this together, right?
38. Harding, "Speaking is Believing," 44, 45.
39. Harding, "Speaking is Believing," 48.
40. Harding, "Speaking is Believing," 54, 57, 59.

end? Apart from her work-related interests, the ritual contraption may have solicited a compulsion to go along and see it through.

In any event, the significance of sequence is not to be found simply in the meaning of the words, but in the beguiling interaction of speaking and listening. Formalization manifests a power that discourages us from deviation in the middle of a sequence. Refusing to participate in rituals is not always a viable option. The Cantonese funeral ritual must be completed to settle the spirit of the deceased. Dracula must be destroyed. Melvin Campbell must be allowed to give witness to his most authentic moments.[41] The dangers of failing to perform the prescribed rituals are by no means modest. In each case a possible eternity is disturbed by the threat.

Example 2: Daily Prayer

While some rituals aim to create authority over an individual, others maintain authority by means of social bonding. Heiko Henkel's essay "'Between Belief and Unbelief' Lies the Performance of Salāt" provides us with an example of this second type.[42] Henkel offers an analysis of the role of the Muslim five-times-daily prayer (salāt) which, he argues, provides believers with a resource for strengthening their commitment to Islam without compelling them into a particular interpretation of Islam. Drawing on fieldwork in Istanbul, Turkey, Henkel argues that salāt effectively inserts a fixed point of reference that maintains "a shared discursive framework among religious Muslims."[43]

---

41. "From within born-again culture, this telling [Campbell's witness, which includes the story of his son's death, KM] was the ultimate evidence of belief, Campbell's moment of maximum authenticity." Harding, "Speaking is Believing," 60. Harding's use of the term "maximum authenticity" speaks to the power generated by formalized ritual—the capacity to make ordinary words seem holy.

42. Heiko Henkel, "'Between Belief and Unbelief Lies the Performance of Salāt': Meaning and Efficacy of a Muslim Ritual," *Journal of the Royal Anthropological Institute* 11 (2005), 487–507.

43. Henkel, "Between Belief and Unbelief," 488.

Henkel maintains that salāt is "an enormously important resource for Muslim practitioners in facilitating the generation of community and continuity despite enormous social change."[44] The prayer itself is a highly choreographed bodily discipline through which Turkish Muslims "aim to generate and maintain their commitment to the Islamic tradition."[45] By inserting a sequence of practice into everyday life, practitioners are able to integrate a diversity of interpretative traditions and subjectivities while at the same time enacting an "unequivocal commitment to Islam" and an "affirmation of Muslim community across different interpretations of Islam."[46]

Henkel illustrates this point with reference to an evening out with three married couples.[47] The account begins with the separate socializing of women and men giving the evening "a particular *dindar* (religious) Muslim character." The host, Hakan, then asked his male guests, Hüsameddin (a lecturer in history) and Sahin (an economist), if they had already performed the evening salāt. Having not done so, the three retreat to the bathroom for ablutions and then to one of the bedrooms of the apartment for the prayer.

As the evening progresses, the conversation touches on Turkey's unfolding economic crisis, the policies of Turkey's governing parties, liberalization and, most contentiously, the relationship between state and religious authority. Henkel indicates that the argument became heated and increasingly animated, much to the discomfort of the host. It was only with difficulty that Hakan was able to stop the intense exchange between Sahin, who accused the Islamist party of abusing religion to gain political power, and Hüsameddin, who countered by saying that the problem in Turkey was religious leaders abusing their positions as religious authorities by interfering with politics.

After a modest recounting of some of the details of this conversation, Henkel turns to the role of salāt. He observes that "the three young men clearly share neither a coherent ideology nor an organization, and their ways of life are shaped by a multitude of heterogeneous

---

44. Henkel, "Between Belief and Unbelief," 488.
45. Henkel, "Between Belief and Unbelief," 489.
46. Henkel, "Between Belief and Unbelief," 489.
47. Henkel, "Between Belief and Unbelief," 490–492.

institutions, disciplines, and social networks." However, "they are united in a shared, although normally unstated, commitment. It is here—in defining, reaffirming, and making explicit the shared commitment of Muslim practitioners to the precepts of the Islamic tradition—that the salāt provides these practitioners with a powerful resource."[48] The ritual is a resource for Muslim unity.[49]

While Henkel is impressed by the way the ritual facilitates this shared commitment, he adds that there was also a disciplinary intention underlying the meeting. Hakan and his friends were worried that Sahin had become somewhat lax in his religious commitment. The evening was arranged in the hope that the influence of his friends would strengthen that commitment.[50] Henkel maintains that the performance of the ritual does not resolve conflicting interpretations. Instead, "it introduces an objective criterion for assessing virtue as it marks the dividing line between believers (müminin) and others."[51]

Without reiterating the extensive details of Henkel's account, the five-times-daily prayers consist of a number of prayer-cycles which consist of a sequence of stations. Someone familiar with the prayer-cycles can perform the intricate prayer in a few minutes. The main themes of the prayer affirm God's magnificence, as well as the singularity and truth of the revelation received by Muhammad. Prior to being performed, the practitioner and the space must be in a state of ritual purity.[52] The result is the creation of "a ritual sphere with a clearly demarcated interior" that "temporarily turns any office, any living room, any street-corner, into a mosque as well as any office-clerk into a Muslim."[53] The prayer, Henkel argues, is explicit and straightforward: "the practitioner affirms his or her commitment to the truth of the Qur'anic revelation and submission to the command of God."[54]

---

48. Henkel, "Between Belief and Unbelief," 491.

49. Henkel does not address the question of gender when it comes to Muslim unity.

50. Henkel, "Between Belief and Unbelief," 492.

51. Henkel, "Between Belief and Unbelief," 492.

52. For details see Henkel, "Between Belief and Unbelief," 492–496.

53. Henkel, "Between Belief and Unbelief," 497.

54. Henkel, "Between Belief and Unbelief," 496.

In analyzing the effect of the prayer, Henkel argues that salāt "establishes a web of social relations mediated by commitment to a shared discursive framework" that can be seen to "define a transnational Muslim community."[55] This practice is not unlike singing a national anthem. Enacted belief becomes the medium of a shared sense of identity and common language through which to articulate agreement or dissent about particular social projects. The ritual operates as a funnel of sorts, channeling what would otherwise be an entropic linguistic diffusion into an affective sense of common ground and unity amidst historical and political diversity. Non-participation is tantamount to rejection, not simply of the ritual, but rejection of common ground itself.

It should be noted, in reading Henkel's essay alongside Bloch's the reader will be promoted to draw different conclusions. Henkel argues that the "shared discursive framework" sustained by the ritual practice of prayer does not commit participants to a particular political or religious project but instead affirms the shared language and resources of Islam as a mutual starting point.[56] While we can agree with this in part, we can also see in the context of Bloch's understanding of formalization that this commitment to a shared normative identity, strengthened by means of ritual, demarcates a remarkably stringent limitation. Only those participating in the ritual are included in the shared language and resources of Islam. Henkel indicates that the ritual is a boundary between belief and unbelief, believer and unbeliever. This boundary is maintained by the ritual yet, when viewed alongside Bloch, prompts us to see the function of the ritual differently.

Interestingly, Henkel starts his article by mentioning his friend Ayeçan, a middle-aged professional woman from Ankara and "self-declared secularist" who finds the prayer's "dramatic gesture of submission" to be proof of an "irrationality" and "intolerance." Henkel indicates that he hopes to convince his "secularist Muslim" friend that the performance of salāt facilitates new and innovative

---

55. Henkel, "Between Belief and Unbelief," 500.

56. Henkel freely uses the term religion and it is in the context of his essay that it is repeated here.

interpretations of Islam even while retaining a "shared discursive framework of a community of believers."[57] However, as his own account of the ritual shows—those who do not participate may fall into the category of unbeliever.[58] The shared discursive regime that Henkel claims is present for practitioners is decidedly absent in this context.

The ritual here does seem to reproduce the (perceived) authority of a shared discursive framework. However, the reproduced framework is not a universal or neutral starting point, even if it leaves open the possibility of multiple interpretations of the Islamic tradition. When we consider the wider context, the ritual participates in the reproduction of a particular kind of Muslim identity. That Henkel identifies his friend as a secularist *Muslim* suggests that a salāt practitioner is not the only kind of Muslim one can be. As Henkel indicates, the performance of salāt creates a razor-sharp division between those desiring to signal a particular kind of commitment to Islam and those who do not. It is the marking and maintaining of a particular kind of identity and a particular kind of authority. By misreading the inclusive and exclusive power of the ritual, Henkel also misreads the dangers of refusing to participate.

While Henkel argues that the ritual inserts a fixed point of reference—a space that transcends local particularities by creating a transcendental community—reading Henkel with Bloch suggests we produce a more nuanced account. The ritual, by means of its fixed features, generates the illusion of transcendence or the illusion of a shared discursive field precisely by means of reduction. In other words, the ritual makes its symbols appear holy and powerful because they have been stripped of interpretive options. This illusion of transcendence then makes it appear as though the "shared discursive framework" is operative, even if it is not. It is this illusionary quality, the very nature of its power as a ritual, that Henkel misconstrues.[59] Henkel seems to assume that the symbols used within rituals con-

---

57. Henkel, "Between Belief and Unbelief," 487, 503

58. Henkel, "Between Belief and Unbelief," 500–503.

59. To be clear, the power of ritual is both a physical power (in the sense that there is physical compliance) as well as an ideological power (the authorizations prompted or signaled by the ritual).

tain, or at least contour, vast reservoirs of meaning. This assumption is precisely what Bloch's theory of formalization challenges. With this caveat in mind, we are in a better position to see the efficacy of salāt as a ritual that maintains traditional authority, as opposed to opening the door to universality, in a way that facilitates a semblance of common ground without commitment to a particular political project.[60]

The boundary signaled by the practice of salāt is a boundary that demarcates one group from another and gives us a good sense of how rituals reproduce rankings and hierarchies. Despite Henkel's protestations, it may well be that Ayęcan, despite her status as a secularist Muslim, may have a great deal in common with her non-secularist peers—a shared language, sense of place, and common future. There is nothing about the ritual that suggests otherwise. There is nothing about the practice of the ritual that suggests that one group is more or less kindred than the other. These details are not resolved in the context of ritual performance, but in the context of debate and discussion. Nevertheless, and this is the power of ritual, the line between believer and unbeliever is drawn and made clear. The threat to unity appears to be magically suspended on the practice of salāt, also revealing a complex range of dangers and aversions for participants and non-participants alike.

Example 3: Exhumations

Bruce Lincoln's essay "Revolutionary Exhumations in Spain" provides us with a good example of ritual in the service of social critique—the dissolution of authority.[61] As Lincoln notes, the exhumation of

---

60. Henkel is ambiguous on this point. At times he indicates that this shared discursive framework is open ended (as he tries to convince his secularist Muslim friend). At other times he suggests it works only to maintain commonality among "religious Muslims." Henkel, "Between Belief and Unbelief,"488. As is evident, I disagree with the former and agree with the latter, with the qualification that this commonality is provincial.

61. Bruce Lincoln, "Revolutionary Exhumations in Spain," *Discourse and the Construction of Society*, 2nd edition (Chicago, IL: University of Chicago Press, 2014), 105–127.

corpses in Spain created a macabre spectacle that has confused scholars for years. By situating the ritual in the larger context of anticlericalism, he hopes to better understand its power and appeal. For our purposes here, the ritual exhumation of corpses provides an example of a symbolic critique of church authorities with a provocative evocation of strong sentiments.[62]

In the era of the Second Republic (1931–1939), Spain was divided into two mutually hostile segments. These groups can be broadly construed, albeit not entirely accurately, as the anticlerical Left and the Catholic Church-supporting Right.[63] Between 1931 and 1936, three elections had taken place—won respectively by the Left, then the Right, then the Left. These elections were characterized by increasingly violent actions and deepening estrangements between the various segments in society. In July 1936, army officers sympathetic to the Right staged a ritual *pronunciamiento* (a pronouncement from the military) declaring the Left to have lost the ability to maintain order. Historically this announcement, accompanied by a show of force, had been successful. This time, it failed. The government took the unprecedented action of distributing arms to labor federations and anarcho-syndicalists (groups sympathetic to the working classes). The workers confronted and defeated the army in major cities and took the opportunity to enact their own rituals of re-creation. Lincoln contends the Left attempted to "dismantle the bourgeois social, political, and economic order" in order to "construct a radically egalitarian, militantly solidary working-class society in its place."[64] He writes:

> Overnight the rules and habits of centuries dissolved, and a sweeping transformation in the conduct of human relations was accomplished. Suits and neckties disappeared, and overalls became the preferred dress. Women took to the streets and catcalls were forgotten. Waiters

---

62. "Discourse is not only an instrument of persuasion, operating along rational (or pseudorational) and moral (or pseudomoral) lines, it is also an instrument of sentiment evocation." Ideological persuasion and sentimental evocation have "the capacity to shape and reshape society itself." Lincoln, "Introduction," *Discourse and the Construction of Society*, 7.

63. Lincoln, "Revolutionary Exhumations in Spain," 105.

64. Lincoln, "Revolutionary Exhumations in Spain," 107.

stared customers in the eye and spoke to them as equals. Bootblacks refused tips as signs of condescension and charity. But also, those identified too closely with the Right stood exposed to terror and repression, being deprived of the norms and institutions that had previously protected them. In particular, throughout that portion of Spain where the rising was defeated, churches were burned, priests were shot, and works of religious art were shattered.[65]

The most striking action taken against the Church, however, was a "macabre spectacle that was played out in numerous towns and cities: the exhumation and public display of the long-buried corpses of priests, nuns and saints some of whom had been naturally mummified by the dry Spanish heat."[66] The responses to the exhumations varied. There is evidence that some on the Left clowned or masqueraded with the skeletons, finding the spectacle amusing. The Right, meanwhile, circulated grisly photographs and described the events as inhumane, barbaric, and bestial. Liberal historians, Lincoln writes, identified the events as a "regrettable excess perpetrated by uncontrollable fanatics in the heat of a crisis."[67]

While the spectacle does not seem to have much in common with highly orchestrated ceremonies or disciplined routines, it does contain a semblance of symbolic power. This power, as Lincoln illustrates in his analysis, is that of critique by means of the evocation of sentiment, however ambiguous. In Lincoln's view, the exhumation of corpses enacts a "profanophany," or an assault and mockery of the transcendent purity of the Church. The display of bodily decomposition is a contrasting and dissembling image in the context of the eternalizing discourse of clerical power. By disturbing the symbolic dead, the ritual is positioned to create a powerful affective response. Participating in the throwing down of idols, the Left was able to enact a radical freedom and create a militant solidarity, while simultaneously exposing the powerlessness of the Church and its supporters. It is also an act that allows no hope of reconciliation.[68]

---

65. Lincoln, "Revolutionary Exhumations in Spain," 107.
66. Lincoln, "Revolutionary Exhumations in Spain," 107–108.
67. Lincoln, "Revolutionary Exhumations in Spain," 111.
68. Lincoln, "Revolutionary Exhumations in Spain," 116–125.

Like most rituals, the exhumation of corpses is ambiguous. Any meaning we attribute to the ritual must be carefully circumscribed by its context. Following Bloch, the key question is not what the ritual means but how it performs—what it does. The range of responses includes everything from horror and disgust to entertainment and hilarity. Unlike fundamentalist witnessing, which is deployed primarily in the context of the unsaved, and unlike salāt, which is a daily ritual, the exhumation of corpses was not intended to become a routine. It was a strategic deployment of powerful symbols to create an irrevocable affect. In this instance, it appears as though the Left was utilizing dangers and aversions in order to propagate a vision of a new beginning.

Conclusion

Rituals are among the primary means through which we create, maintain, and dissolve authority. In Bloch's reading, rituals are vehicles of authority, authorization, and social control. They create powerful moods and affects that influence the ambient social and political network of interpersonal relations and offer an experience of meaning-less eternity within an otherwise meaning-full ordinary state of affairs. As such, rituals play a crucial part in producing, reproducing, and transforming social norms, institutions, as well as acceptable and unacceptable forms of rhetoric and discourses. Rituals are lynchpins of dangers and aversions.

In the examples above, we see the ritual of witnessing aiming to bring about the highest possible good of evangelical Christianity—the salvation of the soul and the realization of God's will on Earth. The ritual of salāt is thought to participate in the reproduction of proper Muslim identities within a society conflicted by community tensions between the secular and the religious. And finally, we see a ritual used to create a chasm between one segment of the population and another, a chasm that divides groups into those who are realizing radical egalitarian freedom in history and those who accept the false claims of a corrupt institution merely slouching towards eternity. In each instance, whether by means of creating authority, maintaining authority, or dissolving authority, rituals are used to create boundaries and borders between groups: saved and unsaved, believer and unbeliever, free and unfree. Formalization and ritual shift and organize so that we can see who fits where. These rituals demarcate who is in and who is out, what is dangerous and what should be avoided, and even how structures can be challenged.

In this sense, rituals are perceived to contribute to the realization of a particular vision of the good or bad life. As Lincoln argues, rituals participate in the construction of society. They are vehicles or architectures of thought and action as much as they are instruments of thought and action. This dyadic character of ritual should help us see rituals as special forms of communication that not only focus action and attention but also connect in a variety of ways with a larger social and historical context of ordinary communication and social exchange. Bloch's conception of ritual, however, does not need to be reduced or streamlined into condensed segments of interaction. Indeed, his theory contains the kernels for further exploring system features of society. Settler colonialism, for example, could be viewed as a highly formalized and racist system of interaction that generates a pervasive sense in the mind and body of the settler that Indigenous populations constitute "matter out of place."[69] Bloch's understanding of ritualization might account for "settlers' continuing need to obliterate people."[70] The capacity of formalization to make symbols and contexts appear eternal would be an ideal vehicle for erasing the past and making unsettling features of the present invisible.

As I hope is clear, formalization's power is not in explaining or describing or giving meaning. Formalization describes a process through which options of expression and action are *reduced*. This conception of ritual is broad, including everything from etiquette

---

69. McCallum and Perry, *Structures of Indifference*, 130. With reference to Judge Timothy Preston's final report on the death of Brian Sinclair, McCallum and Perry write it is as if "his very presence and being were, in part, to blame; that is, he just simply should not have been there or perhaps simply should not have been at all."

70. McCallum and Perry, *Structures of Indifference*, 6. McCallum and Perry are referencing the work of Sherene Razack, *Dying from Improvement* (Toronto: University of Toronto Press, 2015).

to extreme forms of religious authority. Focusing on ritual gives us insight into permissions and authorizations as the means through which actions become automatic and compulsory. Rituals can preserve our classifications and challenge them. In the end, Bloch's theory of ritual helps us understand why Dracula had to be annihilated, even against good conscience. Each step of Dracula's destruction was achieved by means of ritual. But if you know in advance that ritual locks you into a sequence of action that will be difficult to avoid, why start? Well, that's what stories are for.

Chapter 4

Myths and Mythmaking

One of the more innovative developments in the study of myth comes out of Willi Braun and Russell T. McCutcheon's *Guide to the Study of Religion*. What I find particularly compelling about McCutcheon's chapter on "Myth" is that it asks us to shift our attention away from the content of myth and toward its curation. For McCutcheon, the study of myth is directed not by some predetermined content but by the form, and that form invariably conceals the social interests underlying its curation. Myth *presents*. In the manufacturing of myth, mythmakers make use of assumptions and associations in order to manipulate the social fabric, often hiding their own tracks along the way. Because of the creative power and flexibility of myth, mythmakers are primary purveyors of dangers and aversions.

McCutcheon starts the chapter with a few observations. Most people using the word myth make some rather modernist assumptions, "that one can somehow perceive and distinguish between *reality as it really is*, on the one hand, and *reality as it happens to be (mis) represented*, on the other."[1] McCutcheon notes that myth is most often discussed as either a false representation of reality or as a prescientific account of events in the world. The wide range of books starting with titles such as *Seven Myths of* or *Seven Myths about* are usually good examples of how the term myth is used to describe something that is false, with a more corrective view outlined in each of the seven chapters.[2] When not describing myth as something explicitly false,

---

1. Russell T. McCutcheon, "Myth," in Braun and McCutcheon, eds., *Guide to the Study of Religion* (New York: Continuum, 2000), 190.

2. See, for example, Paul Jentz, *Seven Myths of Native American History* (Indianapolis, IN: Hackett Publishing, 2018). These books are often excellent, and Jentz's is a brilliant critique of attitudes and practices that perpetuate violence

many introductory volumes define the term as denoting prescientific stories that seek to explain otherwise mysterious events in the world, such as creation, death, misfortune, or reproduction.[3] Both uses present myth in a binary fashion. On the one side we have myth, and on the other side we have history (or science or truth). Whatever the topic, the subject is framed in such a way that the person using the word "myth" implicitly adopts a position of knowledge, with powers to describe what is real and what is not, what is to be avoided, and what is dangerous. As McCutcheon puts it, both uses of the term shelter an intellectual commitment to a particular distinction between fact and fiction, truth and falsehood, story and science.[4] This distinction might be less problematic as a proposal rather than as a presupposition.

As mentioned, McCutcheon's redescription of myth focuses less on its content and more on its curation. The mythmaker can be an academic, architect, cleric, politician, or storyteller using any number of mediums for advancing their interests. Mythmaking refers to media of presentation that manipulate and organize or reorganize systems of rank and classification. Mythmaking is an activity that asserts values, identity, and collectivity. Myths also invariably advance the social interests of its purveyors.[5]

An example of mythmaking I like to use in class concerns self-presentation. When we are asked, "What did you do this morning?,"

---

against Indigenous peoples, but they are not using or aiming to develop a more critical account of myth.

3. For a quick overview, see Robert A. Segal, "Myth and Science," *Myth: A Very Short Introduction*, 2nd edition (Oxford: Oxford University Press, 2015), 10–29.

4. McCutcheon, "Myth," 191. I would distinguish between a naïve intellectual commitment, which simply makes the distinction between fact and fiction without comment, and a self-reflective intellectual commitment, which makes the distinction explicit and addresses the issues and problems raised by the assumption. Most of the time, myth is deployed in the naïve sense.

5. "If we are to treat myth as an ideological ... discourse, we will need a more dialectic, eminently political theory of narration, one that recognizes the capacity of narrators to modify details of the stories that pass through them, introducing changes in the classificatory order as they do so, most often in ways that reflect their subject position and advance their interests." Lincoln, *Theorizing Myth*.

how might we respond? What kind of morning do we try to sell the person asking the question? Here's one narrative: "Up and at 'em, coffee in hand, ready to write by 9 a.m." It's a good story—very intellectual superhero! Here's a second narrative: "I watched the kids make their own breakfast while looking blurry-eyed out the window at the bird feeder, coffee in hand. I stacked the breakfast dishes in the sink. Moving to my workstation, I dropped a stack of articles on the floor and spent 30 minutes sorting them out. Annoyed by the waste of time, I checked email on my phone for 20 minutes and then played a video game for 35 minutes. I edited one paragraph of my book and then refilled my coffee cup. Bathroom break. Is it lunch yet? Better check that video game again, the grinding never ends." The first narrative is a concise and idealizing story about how one might want to be perceived. It sells a particular kind of character. The second narrative is equally idealizing, selling a different kind of character. Narration can't avoid participating in idealizations of one sort or another. But we should keep in mind, myth isn't special. Mythmaking is the ordinary way in which we make sense of things to ourselves and to others, but we should not let the ordinariness of myth get in the way of seeing its extensive power to shape, frame, and renegotiate boundaries.[6]

To put it in now-familiar terms of magic, myth is also a calibration or recalibration of perceived essences, which is why, more often than not, mythmaking and classification go hand in hand.[7] Myth can define what counts and what doesn't count as reality (or what counts or doesn't count as "deeper" reality). One of my favorite examples of mythmaking has to do with a momentous event in 2012. It was an event that caused a tremor in the social fabric, a great disturbance in our social imagination. I am referring, of course, to Disney's multi-billion dollar purchase of Lucasfilm. Shortly after the acquisition of copyright, representatives at Disney made the stunning

---

6. My very favorite study of mythmaking in the service of social formation is the recently revised Kelly J. Baker, *The Zombies are Coming* (Chapel Hill, NC: Blue Crow Books, 2020).

7. For some insights on this relation, see Bruce Lincoln's comments in *Theorizing Myth*, 146–147.

announcement that the events written about in the 100+ *Star Wars* novels would no longer be considered canonical. Luke Skywalker would no longer be married to Mara Jade. In effect, Disney used the symbolic powers of copyright to recalibrate the canon and give themselves creative freedom in the upcoming movie sequels. While those who are not fans of the Star Wars universe may not have even noticed, the shift within Star Wars fandom was enormous. Suddenly, what was fictively real within an imaginary world became fictively not real.[8]

It is through the power of mythmaking that canon and authority are contoured and given status. The maneuvering of the legal fictions of canon are accomplished by means of myth, often concealing the authority of the mythmaker. Why, for example, do copyright holders have authority when it comes to the fictive reality of imaginary worlds? This is why focusing on the myth—the once real but now legendary marriage of Mara Jade and Luke Skywalker, for example—is largely pointless. When it comes to myth and mythmaking, separating text and context reproduces a problem Maurice Bloch detected within the study of ritual. When we ignore the context of a sequence of social actions by focusing on the meaning of symbols used in those actions, we become purveyors of mystification.

In our context, myth is the means through which the rose becomes imbued with passion, the corpse handler with the status of an impure pariah, or the cup with impurity.[9] This conception of mythmaking

---

8. Discussed in my essay "The Ion *Canon* Will Fire Several Shots to Make Sure Any Enemy Ships Will be Out of Your Flight Path: Canonization, Tribal Theologians, and Imaginary World Building," in John Lyden and Ken Derry, eds., *The Myth Awakens: Canon, Conservatism, and Fan Reception of Star Wars* (Eugene, OR: Cascade Books, 2018), 147–162.

9. Just to draw this out, there are always competing mythmakers. In the case of the Cantonese villages, the village women circulate their own interpretation of death rituals and death pollution in competition with the authority of the priests, but must do so in a subtle way so as to not draw attention to their own expertise. The priests advance their own version of death pollution in alignment with their interest to preserve their authority in the face of the distrust and disdain of the villagers (and so on). James L. Watson, *Village Life in Hong Kong* (Hong Kong: Chinese University Press, 2004), 397–399.

directs our attention away from an exclusive emphasis on the content of a story, discourse, or structure and towards its design and designer. Mythmaking is a process of social formation—of manipulating, creating, and struggling with the organization of human relationships. McCutcheon explains that myth as mythmaking is an ordinary means we use to fashion and authorize worlds: values are enshrined, hierarchies set up, and contradictions concealed.[10] In my view, mythmaking is how we constitute and frame what Bloch calls the "transcendental social," how we come to see and experience a social imaginary world as real.

The advantage of McCutcheon's conception of myth is that it does not privilege the position of the scholar as arbiter of reality, since no one is exempt from this kind of activity. As Bruce Lincoln argues, scholarship is myth with footnotes.[11] Myth tells us what to focus on by establishing meaningful correspondences between things. It's design work. In the novel *Dracula*, Dracula becomes a monster by means of the extensive mythmaking labor of Abraham Van Helsing. His almost unquestioned authority is as key to Dracula's annihilation as are his wild tales about vampires. The execution of Dracula is set up by the mythmaker Van Helsing and reinforced by rituals prescribed within the myths he spins.[12]

In other words, if ritual is a formalized process through which particular symbols come to appear as holy, mythmaking is the discursive

---

10. McCutcheon, "Myth," 200.

11. Lincoln, *Theorizing Myth*, 209. "If myth is ideology in narrative form, then scholarship is myth with footnotes." I would further add that footnotes are not limited to literary form. Oral traditions often track sources and locations. See Gregory Younging, *Elements of Indigenous Style* (Edmonton: Brush, 2018).

12. I am not revalorizing or revisiting a conception of myth and ritual that suggests rituals act out myth. Myths are discourses that shape the social field. Rituals are instances of reductions within that social field. There are formal and formalizing elements within the activity of mythmaking. The relation is not one of origins but of conceptual interaction and thematic focus for analytic purposes. In other words, the relation between myth and ritual should be viewed as a theoretical relation. Th scholar of myth asks questions about how collectives are formed. The scholar of ritual asks questions about how utterances appear powerful.

process of elevating or nominating symbols as candidates for ritualization. As we saw in the previous chapter, witnessing is a ritual that establishes authority over a particular individual. But the symbols used within that process are circumscribed by myth: birth, rebirth, water and blood, sacrifice and atonement. Rituals work on the basis of the reduction of meaning and the reduction of options in terms of language and interaction. Formalization channels action in a particular direction but is not conducive to the creation of shared imaginary worlds. Ritual lacks the creativity and flexibility required to respond to the ebb and flow of the everyday conflict of interpretations—the border work of managing values and social groupings.

The difference between the modernist conception of myth described by McCutcheon and a more critical conception of myth as mythmaking is the subject of one of my class assignments. I ask students to read several theories of myth and apply what they have learned to a superhero comic book (usually *Captain Marvel*, *Ms. Marvel*, or *Black Panther*). When using a modernist theory of myth, such as Karen Armstrong's, students write about the conflict between good and evil, the mysteries of life and death, and the power of story to transform.[13] Greg Garrett's *Holy Superheroes!* is a good example of how to read superhero comics using a modernist theory of myth. According to Garrett, superheroes become mirrors of the sacred in which we can see, and to some degree model, our own activities.[14]

After reading McCutcheon and the works of Bruce Lincoln, however, students begin to notice different things. They notice and comment on advertisements, copyright, and page count. By turning away from an exclusive concern with the graphic narrative content of a comic book, we begin to learn a great deal about packaging, marketing, movie tie-ins, casting decisions, and production value—all of

---

13. Karen Armstrong, *A Short History of Myth* (Toronto: Vintage, 2006). Armstrong views myth as a universal vehicle for dealing with the contingencies of life. For Armstrong, myths are not simply cultural expressions and strategies for dealing with the complexities of life but also manifestations of the sacred within history.

14. Greg Garrett, *Holy Superheroes!*, revised and expanded edition (Louisville, KY: Westminster John Knox Press, 2008).

which are rendered invisible in the modernist conception of myth. Just as Heiko Henkel was taken in by the way in which ritual presents itself as powerful and holy, Armstrong too enters into the narrative and envisions herself as a character within that world. A more critical conception of myth asks us to take a step back and look at the style of the myth, the design activity of mythmaking rather than the marvelous tale itself.

In the last chapter, we reviewed Bloch's question concerning how symbols become powerful. The question for McCutcheon is this: How is it that human beings accomplish the trick of coming together and acting collectively over great spans of time and space?[15] It's a question of how narratives fabricate groups or essential identities (which rituals can then signal). Following Roland Barthes, McCutcheon suggests that myth should not be decontextualized with an emphasis on its message but should be contextualized "by the way in which it utters its message."[16] Myth, or mythmaking, is the means through which certain things become meaningful and other things are left to the side. Mythmaking is "the ongoing process of constructing, authorizing and reconstructing social identities or social formations," and the study of mythmaking entails the creation of a "catalog of strategies for *maintaining* paradoxes, *fighting* over dissonances, and *surviving* [and recovering from] breakdowns."[17] For McCutcheon, the study of myth is the study of how human beings make and reproduce meaning by means of facilitating moments of joint or shared intentionality, the means through which collectives are formed and reproduced with specific reference to the extraordinary, the transcendental, the ideal, or idealizing. Put another way, mythmaking is the business of making "particular and contingent worldviews appear to be ubiquitous and absolute."[18] It is through myths and mythmaking that dangers and aversions are created, maintained, and contested.

A subtle but telling example of an attempt to make the contingent appear absolute can be found in the work of Richard Dawkins, whom

---

15. McCutcheon, "Myth," 201.

16. Barthes quoted in McCutcheon, "Myth," 201. Emphasis removed.

17. Gary Lease quoted in McCutcheon, "Myth," 203.

18. William Arnal quoted McCutcheon, "Myth," 205.

I mentioned earlier. In *The Greatest Show on Earth*, Dawkins recounts an interview with an anti-evolutionist. Frustrated by a position that has little or no interest in science, Dawkins eventually tells the interviewer to "go to the museums and look at the facts and don't believe what you have been told that there is no evidence. Just go and look at the evidence ... Just open your eyes and look at the facts."[19] Dawkins suggests that all the evidence we need to accept the reality of evolution can be seen in a museum with a decent display of the fossil record. If we see the bones, the scales will fall from our eyes. All we have to do is look, and we will know. What this seeing-and-knowing myth obscures is the intensive and exhaustive labor of countless scientists and scholars who have been arguing and debating about evolution for years. While his frustration is understandable, it is somewhat ironic that Dawkins opts to conceal the complex history of theorizing with an appeal to visual revelation.[20]

Another example can be found in the volume *UFO Crash at Roswell* with contributions by Benson Saler, Charles Ziegler, and Charles Moore. The book begins with an historical account of the Roswell narratives. In the first chapter by Charles Ziegler, after an historical account, six versions of the Roswell myth are outlined. The versions, in varying degrees of detail, describe an encounter with extraterrestrials. Ziegler tracks the chronological development of each version of the Roswell narrative and notes changes and offers and explanation in each case. The chapter is richly documented and each version is assigned an approximate date and a number.[21] Six versions, six myths. When I discuss this in class, however, I always speak of seven myths. Using McCutcheon's definition of myth, the initial true record of the facts, the historical account, is also a myth (with footnotes). McCutcheon's conception does not rely on a distinction between

---

19. Richard Dawkins, *The Greatest Show on Earth* (New York: Free Press, 2009), 202.

20. For an essay dealing with this kind of myth in introductory courses, see Jonathan Z. Smith, "The Necessary Lie: Duplicity in the Disciplines," in Russell T. McCutcheon, *Studying Religion: An Introduction* (London: Equinox, 2007), 73–80.

21. Charles A. Zeigler, "Mythogenesis," in Benson Saler, Charles A. Ziegler, and Charles B. Moore, *UFO Crash at Roswell* (Washington, DC: Smithsonian Books, 2010), 1–29.

myth and history, true and false. We should also draw attention to how McCutcheon's account of myth as mythmaking is itself also a myth, designed to rank and classify and highlight some features instead of others.

Just as Bloch's conception of formalization resides on a spectrum that includes everything from etiquette and political rhetoric to highly orchestrated ritual, mythmaking conceived in this way allows us to expand the scope of the study of myth beyond stories about deities and heroes into a wide range of human activity including any of the meaning-making arts. This critical conception of mythmaking tracks and maps the means through which we not only make the world around us intelligible (whether a theory of evolution or stories about alien visitors) but also remove the historicity of this intelligibility by concealing the complicated work that has gone into the design process. Another key lesson to be learned here is that our myths, with or without footnotes, are under constant revision. The messy contingencies of life require that stories be tweaked for new audiences and changing circumstances. This editing and curating process is the everyday social and political work of making-meaning and, of course, a primary means through which dangers and aversions are negotiated and renegotiated.

As McCutcheon critically observes, the history of scholarship on myth is filled with scholars who argue that myths are reservoirs of the transcendent and transhistorical. Myths described in this way refer to the most important or sacred values of a community and should therefore be held as stories outside the realm of politics. In McCutcheon's view, such scholars not only become mythmakers themselves but also demonstrate how a fixation on the content of a narrative misses out on the scope and function of what we're calling mythmaking. These scholars tend to conceal their own interests and commitments in the mythmaking process. Contrarily, as McCutcheon puts it, it isn't that we find our most important values in myth, but that we fabricate our most important values by means of myth.[22]

Another use of myth can be seen in Niigaan Sinclair's disturbing yet brilliant story about settler colonialism. In the story, a family is

---

22. McCutcheon, "Myth," 199.

greeted by a man with a crown at their door. They invite him in and offer him a cup of tea. He tells the family to move into the bathroom. The family resists but is soon forced into the bathroom, imprisoned, and tortured for over a century. During this time, the family makes a life, as best they can, and listens to everything happening around them. When the bathroom door is finally opened, everything has been changed and the people occupying the house claim it is their house. When questioned about this, the occupiers say that the family should be happy with their space in the bathroom.

The story is part of the CBC series "Beyond 94," which aims to monitor the journey of reconciliation since the publication of the Truth and Reconciliation Commission final report.[23] The TRC report was formed as a reckoning with the devastation caused by Canada's residential school system, but we can see that Sinclair isn't simply monitoring the path to reconciliation. His narrative is a challenge that exceeds the findings and the mandate of the TRC by raising the one thing the TRC was designed to avoid: stolen lands.[24] Sinclair's story continues:

> Then, one day, a well-dressed man who looks like the one with the crown comes up to you.
> He says sorry for everything. That he regrets things have turned out this way. That he hopes your people and his people can reconcile. That a new relationship is possible.
> You ask for your home back. To share at the very least.
> "I'm not that sorry," he says, walking away.
> Turning to the door, you remember the knock.
> And refuse to go away.[25]

While Sinclair's narrative takes the form of myth, at least according to McCutcheon's definition, it is also a myth that lays bare the power

---

23. 94 refers to the 94 Calls to Action published in the final report.

24. See Rachel Yacaaʔał George, "Inclusion is Just the Canadian Word for Assimilation," in Kiera L. Ladner and Myra J. Tait, eds., *Surviving Canada* (Winnipeg: ARP Books, 2017), 49–62.

25. Niigaan Sinclair, "What Reconciliation Feels Like to People 'Locked in the Bathroom' for a Century," March 19, 2018, retrieved June 25, 2021, from www.cbc.ca/news/indigenous/opinion-reconciliation-beyond94-1.4578359.

and violence of the settler colonial myth. The myth isn't simply about heroes and villains, but part of an unfolding path towards reconciliation moving beyond the findings of the Truth and Reconciliation Commission of Canada in 2015. As I hope is evident, the story isn't just a story—it's part of an ongoing relationship, like any myth.[26]

As I have been suggesting through this chapter, it is simple to see how mythmaking relates to dangers and aversions. Mythmaking is one of the many means we have to create and maintain bonds of solidarity, whether by passing along norms from generation to generation or rapidly elevating or devaluing elements within a hierarchy or classification schema. Mythmakers trade in the ordering and reordering of facts, values, and norms. Myths, by means of their presentation, confront us with storied realities. In doing so, myth models "proper" conduct and "proper" perspective on what is good, what is bad, what is to be drawn near, and what is to be avoided. While rituals are often prescribed for remedying dangers and aversions, myths participate in the reckoning of what counts and doesn't count as dangerous in the first place.

For the sake of circumscribing an area of study, McCutcheon thematically distinguishes myth from narrative by identifying mythmaking as a strategy or technique of transformation that fabricates or imagines the extraordinary out of the ordinary. The distinction will not hold for long, but for the moment, it helps focus our study on mythmaking that speaks of transcendence and eternity. The following examples provide three ways in which myths and mythmaking shape and reshape collective identities. The first refers to supernatural assault narratives circulated within evangelical Christianity in Australia and how storytelling is used to exclude competing explanations for events in the world. The second example concerns the narratives that developed and sustain sati veneration and model womanhood in Rajasthan. The third focuses on the many myths of androcentrism and the overlapping and complex ways in

---

26. Truth and Reconciliation Commission of Canada, *Final Report of the Truth and Reconciliation Commission of Canada. Volume One: Summary. Honouring the Truth, Reconciling for the Future* (Toronto: Lorimer, 2015).

which the practices and perspectives of patriarchy and fraternity are reproduced.

Example 1: Narratives about Evil

Andrew Singleton's essay "No Sympathy for the Devil: Narratives about Evil" is a useful illustration of mythmaking by means of oral narrative.[27] It is also helpful because it puts our heuristic definition of evil to a bit of a test. Singleton's essay deals with stories about the devil that refer to a supernatural conception of evil. Unlike the definition of evil as dangers and aversions at work in this primer, evil in Singleton's essay refers to the harmful workings of a supernatural power. That distinction is important to keep in mind moving forward. Singleton's essay focuses on how storytelling enables and encourages members of a community to narrativize certain kinds of experiences as encounters with the devil. This pedagogy of storytelling uses a stylized vocabulary and standardized plot so as to privilege one interpretation of events and oppose competing interpretations. In Singleton's analysis, stories about the devil clarify and strengthen community identity and, for our purposes here, can rightly be regarded as an example of mythmaking.[28]

Story, according to Singleton, is a narrative about events in the past. Storytelling relies on a selective appropriation of past events and characters; they structure events as having a beginning, middle, and end, doing so in a way that implies causality.[29] Telling a story involves fashioning meanings about the matter being reported by offering a "certain way of perceiving the world which privileges certain interests over others."[30] Storytelling is both a means of representing reality and an ideological means through which people identify with one another and coordinate future activities. Importantly, stories are not

27. Andrew Singleton, "No Sympathy for the Devil: Narratives about Evil," *Journal of Contemporary Religion* 16, no. 2 (2001), 177–191.

28. Singleton, "No Sympathy for the Devil," 177, 178.

29. Singleton, "No Sympathy for the Devil," 180.

30. D. Mumby quoted in Singleton, "No Sympathy for the Devil," 181.

only tools of representation but also formative aspects of our shared identities.[31] Stories create community. Storytelling is a mechanism through which listeners and performers come to collectively narrate themselves as a social and political body. There is a high degree of congruence between Singleton's conception of storytelling and McCutcheon's conception of mythmaking. McCutcheon, however, circumscribes myth and mythmaking in terms of how the extraordinary is conjured out of the ordinary, as opposed to other possible uses of narration—the very theme Singleton is interested in.

Singleton's essay focuses on members of conservative Christian faith groups on an Australian university campus in 1999. He presents three story summaries collected from informants participating in a qualitative study. The stories concern combat narratives between forces of good and forces of evil and attest to the truth of a Christian worldview. The performance and circulation of these narratives, Singleton argues, reproduce and sustain a particular Christian way of seeing the world.[32]

For many Christians, evil is real, tangible, and often personified. The narratives selected by Singleton detail encounters with evil spirits with special powers to act against humans. He distinguishes between demonic affliction, the manipulation of attitudes and behavior (rage, lust, deceitfulness), and supernatural assault, the manipulation of sensory perception ("evil presence").[33] The telling and retelling of combat narratives, stories about harm, and stories about the activities of a malevolent evil entity are preeminent means used by conservative Christians to craft a powerful sense of communal opposition, group solidarity, and boundaries.

In the first of the three stories, a young man suspected of being possessed by demons was invited to a Pentecostal Catholic bible camp. The young man is described as behaving strangely. It was said that he was making odd noises, rolling his eyes, and refusing to attend mass. In the story, a charismatic leader engages in intercessory prayer and exorcises the demon. The second story describes targets of the devil's

---

31. A. P. Kerby discussed in Singleton, "No Sympathy for the Devil," 181.
32. Singleton, "No Sympathy for the Devil," 178, 181.
33. Singleton, "No Sympathy for the Devil," 179.

aggression: the Eucharist, bible study, prayer, and new converts. Also taking place at a bible camp, the narrative outlines a series of disturbances intended to frighten or suspend Christian activities. In the narrative, strange noises, inexplicable footprints, and claw marks were greeted with prayer and perseverance. The third story concerns an attack of night paralysis. It begins with a young woman experiencing an evil presence in her room at night. She prays and cries out to God, commanding the evil to go away in the name of Jesus. She consults with a pastor who confirms the reality of the supernatural assault and its aim to make her afraid. The pastor also affirms her strategy for dealing with this supernatural affliction: prayer and spiritual warfare.[34]

In each of the three stories, Singleton observes how the narrative privileges a Pentecostal or charismatic interpretation of events, effectively excluding other possible interpretations (medical or psychiatric, for example). The narratives do not raise possible splits or rifts within Pentecostal interpretations, instead create a strong and clear sense of opposition. In the telling, evil is obviously evil and the means for securing victory are asserted. In each case, Singleton observes how the stories are ordered in a formulaic way, providing an explanation sympathetic to a Pentecostal perspective for the attack and the use of Christian tactics deemed appropriate to secure triumph. As he notes, storytelling "is not just a way of sense-making and organising memories about an experience":

> it is also a way of communicating to others the very experiences which sustain and create community (attack from, and victory over, evil). In other words, stories do not merely embody a worldview (good and evil at war), they also promote a common-sense way of understanding the world.[35]

Christian activities are uplifted, opponents identified, and the distinction between "us" and "them" is secured. The stories are *presented* and do not invite concern with the historical foibles of the narration.

---

34. Singleton, "No Sympathy for the Devil," 183–187.
35. Singleton, "No Sympathy for the Devil," 188.

In this section, we're focusing on narratives that turn the ordinary into the extraordinary in order to better understand how we construct dangers and aversions. Christian stories about the devil identify dangers and threats to the Christian community. These narratives also recommend remedies and catalogue aversions. The scale of the myth is cosmic, quite literally the entire realm of human encounters with the supernatural forces of Good and Evil.

Example 2: Narratives about Ideals

Lindsey Harlan's "Perfection and Devotion: Sati Tradition in Rajasthan" also brings out the importance of storytelling for the construction and reproduction of meaning.[36] While the case of Pentecostal Christian narratives about evil generate solidarity through a shared sense of opposition, Harlan's analysis offers a network of stories interlocking to create an aspirational ideal—the sacrificial woman.

Harlan notes that she was quite surprised to find that sati veneration was alive and well in the Udaipur area of Rajasthan where she conducted her research in 1984–1985. Sati veneration concerns a range of practices that pay homage to women who have lived up to the storied ideals of self-sacrifice. Having been outlawed, Harlan assumed it would have disappeared. However, the "sati paradigm" continues to develop and thrive as the ideals of motherhood and "the good wife" are espoused and renegotiated by the Rajput women she interviewed.[37] By emphasizing highly charged and ethically inflected storytelling—what we're calling mythmaking—we can see how each of the vows that are part of the sati paradigm contain and transmit

---

36. Lindsey Harlan, "Perfection and Devotion: Sati Tradition in Rajasthan," in John Stratton Hawley, ed., *Sati, the Blessing and the Curse: The Burning of Wives in India* (New York: Oxford University Press, 1994), 79–91.

37. Harlan, "Perfection and Devotion," 79. Harlan's book contains a much more nuanced account of the sati paradigm and the ways in which women negotiate and renegotiate their "tradition" within the context of modernization. Lindsey Harlan, *Religion and Rajput Women* (Berkeley, CA: University of California Press, 1992).

a number of important norms. Particularly significant here are the ideals about "a good woman" (*sati*) and the proper duties of a (Rajput) wife. From the narrated Rajasthani Rajput perspective, "a woman becomes a sati through the acquisition of virtue or goodness—that is, *sat*."[38] Acquiring *sat* is a gradual process with three conceptual stages: *patrivrata* (married woman, one who has made a vow to protect her husband), *sativrata* (a vow a wife makes to join her husband in the afterlife), and *satimata* (transformation of the dying woman into a transcendent female divinity).

According to the narratives shared with Harlan, a wife in the first stage serves her husband by attending to his interests and encouraging him to perform his duties. These activities are amplified by the performance of ritual vows, many of which involve fasting: "By fasting she pleases various deities, who compensate her by protecting her husband and by helping her to be a better *pativrata*."[39] According to this view, if a husband predeceases the wife, she is culpable and can escape suspicion by taking a *sativrata*: "When a woman utters her sati vow, she places herself in the context of a vivid temporal fiction."[40] At this time, the moral heat generated by her life of sacrifice for her husband culminates in a fiery explosion on the funeral pyre of her husband wherein the ashes of both bodies become intermingled, affirming the unity of husband and wife established at their wedding fire.[41] During this stage, the wife is beyond life and possesses special powers to curse and establish prohibitions. The final stage of transformation is into a *satimata* (good mother). The *satimata* is a transcendent being viewed as a moral ideal and model. Satis are referred to in the singular, while the particular features of individual wives are condensed and amalgamated: "there is one sati who possesses many aspects."[42] Harlan further writes:

> the fundamental idea Rajputs have of the sati's death is that it represents a manifestation of the virtue of *sat*, a moral and substantive

38. Harlan, "Perfection and Devotion," 80.
39. Harlan, "Perfection and Devotion," 80.
40. Harlan, "Perfection and Devotion," 81.
41. Harlan, "Perfection and Devotion," 81.
42. Harlan, "Perfection and Devotion," 82.

quality that is inherent but latent in the Rajput *pativrata*. *Sat* causes the pativrata to become a *sativrata* if her husband predeceases her, and it manifests itself in flames, which prove that the woman has been a *pativrata* even as they transform her into a *satimata*.[43]

In the liminal or intermediary stage, when moral heat and power are ascending, a *sativrata* may express their desire to protect a family by means of issuing curses (*srap*) or proscriptions (*ok*). These pronunciations are recounted by means of storytelling. Stories about curses inform us about unacceptable behavior in relation to the duties of a good woman, while proscriptions mark a household for protection. Some of the stories Harlan discusses include curses pronounced upon people who interfere with a woman intending to die as a sati. Others tell of the fury that may be released if the death of the husband is the result of inappropriate conduct, or they concern the consequences of attempts to breach the curse. Harlan observes that curses more often than not punish men for what they have or have not done, but the curses are also instructive and designed to influence the lives of women.[44] They discourage unacceptable behavior and instruct those whom the *sativrata* loves, doing so in a way that facilitates and exemplifies their roles as guardians. These narratives speak of strategies for protecting women, warn of dangers to their well-being, and maintain their status as subjects of agency and change.

The establishing of an *ok* is the means through which a *sativrata* marks a household for protection. Harlan notes that as long as the terms of the proscription are "remembered and respected, the sati, now a *satimata*, will ward off and dispel bad fortune."[45] An *ok* may include bans on the wearing of traditional colors that women wear as brides or those that women wear after giving birth, prohibitions against certain types of jewelry associated with marriage (such as ankle bracelets and various other bracelets and bangles) or rules against using baby cradles. Harlan observes that prohibitions are most often associated with being a wife and mother, as they have

---

43. Harlan, "Perfection and Devotion," 83–84.
44. Harlan, "Perfection and Devotion," 85–86.
45. Harlan, "Perfection and Devotion," 89.

to do with marriage, sexuality, and fertility.[46] Following the prohibitions is considered to be auspicious, and such conduct brings a woman and her household under the protection of the *satimata*. The prohibitions serve as regulated aversions. Some of these aversions are associated with potential dangers while others with commitments and protection.

In Harlan's analysis, sati veneration reinforces and strengthens a legacy of feminine sacrifice within a patriarchal hierarchy. By telling and retelling stories that concern womanly sacrifice, women are able to circulate and renegotiate ideals regarding "good women" and reassert their place and power within a community. They make patriarchy their own, in a sense. The stories highlight treasured values and warn against inappropriate conduct. The stories relate everyday activities to divinities and broadly create a protected sphere fit with dangers and aversions. As Harlan notes, "Sati stands for a way of life, a way of life informed by values that are only slowly changing to suit changing social norms and circumstances."[47]

Example 3: Narratives about Gender

Randi Warne's essay "Gender" in *Guide to the Study of Religion* is a densely packed analysis of the mechanisms of gender, the dyadic division of humans into "women" and "men," and the hierarchical situating of one over the other.[48] The essay is an excellent illustration of the complex lattice work of gender and gendering as well as of cataloguing and mapping mythmaking activity. There is no doubt that gendering is both ancient and cross-cultural. The strategies of gendering, which are embedded and embodied in social practices around the globe, are remarkably extensive in scope and function. While gender norms and practices vary according to time and place, Warne documents a list of strategies to which gender is subject: essentializing, cosmologizing, naturalizing, authorizing, valorizing, idealizing,

---

46. Harlan, "Perfection and Devotion," 89.
47. Harlan, "Perfection and Devotion," 90.
48. Warne, "Gender," 140–154.

normalizing, pathologizing, and problematizing. She writes, "These strategies combine in different ways to deploy gender in specific cultural circumstances. The great variety in the combination of these strategies has contributed to much of the debate and, indeed, confusion about gender as a social practice."[49]

Taking these strategies into account, she further complicates gender by outlining its variations in relation to sex. In the first strategy, sex and gender are construed as homologous, where gender simply translates sex. In this view, gender is an extension of a base or essential sex. In the second iteration, gender and sex are viewed as analogous: sex is natural, gender is cultural. Gender is the social meaning assigned to sex. The third strategy asserts that gender and sex is heterogenous. Neither sex nor gender is natural. In this view, gender work creates sex and posits sex as a natural category.[50]

Warne shows how the historical development of gender has influenced the academic study of religion in Europe and North America, using the example of secularization. In ancient practice, Warne notes, the widespread gender ideology assumed a "one sex/flesh" mode. Citing the work of Thomas Laqueur, the model of humanity was largely that of one sex: masculinity is visible without whereas women are but men turned outside in.[51] Since the late eighteenth century, European cultural practices have been predicated on a "two sex/flesh" model, wherein an oppositional difference is assumed, naturalized, cosmologized, and ontologized. Gender opposition is imagined as fixed and eternal and comes with highly prescribed normative roles that, although frequently transgressed, are reinforced and instantiated in widespread institutional practices.[52] Deviance from these norms is pathologized. Women are imagined as dangerous, deviant women even more so.[53]

---

49. Warne, "Gender," 141.

50. Warne, "Gender," 141–142.

51. Laqueur cited in Warne, "Gender," 143.

52. Warne, "Gender," 144.

53. There are countless examples of this double-edged sword. An example by Pamela Milne is one I often discuss in my classes. Pamela J. Milne, "What Shall We Do With Judith? A Feminist Reassessment of a Biblical Heroine," *Semeia* 62 (1993), 37–58.

This categorization was pressed into service when the European middle class enacted a distinction between home and workplace, effectively creating and prescribing distinctions between the private and public spheres. Although the distinction between the two spheres was itself a renegotiation of culture occurring under the auspices of industrial capitalism, the result was an entrenchment of gender ideals and a variety of associations with each. The public sphere came to be associated with masculinity, science, objectivity, reason, and the dis-embodied male gaze. The private sphere came to be associated with femininity, religion, emotion, subjectivity, and the activities of repro-duction. According to this dichotomous logic, there is a pure mind and an impure body. While exchange and commerce between the two spheres was common (e.g. women took paid employment outside the home), the ideological distortion obscured and elided much comment on these "transgressions."[54] As Warne critically notes, women vig-orously petitioned for the right to vote and to own property, they defended the sanctity of their own bodies and sexualities regarding marriage and reproductive rights, and they fought for the right to education and access to the professions.[55] By refusing to focus on the content and context preferred by an androcentric perspective, Warne is able to discern an incongruence between the idealizing narrative and the context in which the narrative is produced.

Within this eighteenth-century ideological matrix and politi-cal conflict, the scientific study of religion is said to have emerged. Despite a widespread cultural preoccupation with the "Woman Question," gender was not established as an operative category in the study of religion. In other words, the early scholars of religion accepted and perpetuated the many myths of androcentrism. As Warne puts it: "The prescriptive gender ideology of separate spheres, marked by an aggressive, rational, public, culturally authoritative male and a passive, receptive, emotional, private and nurturant female was naturalized, ontologized, and authorized in the scientific study of religion."[56] The separations characteristic of the study of

---

54. Warne, "Gender," 149–150.
55. Warne, "Gender," 150.
56. Warne, "Gender," 150.

religion between scientific and religious thought or between modern and primitive thought, are all gendered. Warne writes, "The symmetry of androcentrism assumes that what men do is of preeminent human importance."[57] This gendered viewpoint takes men as representative of humanity overall, while "what women do is important only in the terms set down for them within the androcentric frame."[58]

From within this masculinist entrenchment in the then-fledgling discipline of religion, the theory of evolution was loosely adopted to serve as a model of the social evolution of secularization: magic, religion, science. As "mankind" moved from childhood to adulthood, rational adults left childish dependence upon religion in the past. This personal journey was mapped with minimal mediation onto peoples and places within the European colonial empire. The glowing achievements of male dominated fields of science, politics, and technological engineering became the highest rung on a civilizational ladder. The assumptions of secularization theory included the primacy of an idealized bourgeois public sphere as normative, the division of labor between church and state as natural, and the notion that Christianity—even if seeming like a remnant of an earlier age—was the most logical and complete religion.[59]

With reference to Ann Braude's study of women and religion in the United States, Warne shows that these measurements of the secular fail to account for the widespread participation of women in religious life—as critics, leaders, and reformers.[60] Women have always participated in public life, but because this participation did not confirm to the androcentric perspective, their contributions have been ignored or treated as anomalous. Studies such as Warne's highlight how the (androcentric) secularization model tells us more about its

---

57. Warne, "Gender," 150–151.

58. Warne, "Gender," 151. Citing Lerner.

59. Warne, "Gender," 151–152.

60. Braude's study of Spiritualism shows how political and religious reforms often walk hand in hand. For example, the chapter "Mediums versus Medical Men" documents women's resistance to (often harmful) male medical practices by means of presenting alternatives to these practices alongside open opposition. Ann Braude, *Radical Spirits: Spiritualism and Women's Rights in Nineteenth-Century America*, 2nd edition (Bloomington, IN: Indiana University Press, 2001).

(androcentric) architects than anything else. If we challenge the androcentric view, the theory of secularization is dislodged and perhaps disappears altogether.[61]

Warne's critical account of the importance of gender is highly revealing of the mythmaking power of androcentrism, a myth that is both in the world and part of or constitutive of the means through which we apprehend the world. Warne argues that, because of masculinist assumptions, the study of religion remains implicated in reproducing mythmaking practices about gender. She further shows how such norms determine and shape what counts and doesn't count as religious, what counts as valuable, and what is ignored. Androcentric narratives have a strong aversion to talking about women in terms other than those of their own misogynist assumptions. From political theory to the study of religion, mothers, sisters, and daughters are excluded from the brotherhood of man.

One of the implications of Warne's critique of the study of religion and its androcentric prejudices is that the study of evil needs a thorough reconsideration. If the concept of evil within the philosophy of religion and within moral philosophy is rooted in androcentric myths, and if evil is coded within these myths as "feminine," it becomes necessary to radically rethink the interests at work underlying the politics of evil. In an earlier version of my class on evil, I included a section on evil and the feminine. I eventually collapsed the section and incorporated it into every part of the course since sex and gender ideologies invariably associate the feminine with dangers and aversions.

Conclusion

This chapter has introduced the concept of mythmaking as a strategy of social formation. Mythmaking has a tendency to conceal its operative function, while simultaneously creating frames of reference and value for social actors. What counts as the "good" and "bad" life is measured and prescribed by the mythmaker in their design and

---

61. Warne, "Gender," 152.

by their circulation of a particular myth. Mythmaking is the means through which we coordinate and organize the social world, how we make things appear and disappear. As we have seen, storytelling can shore up solidarity and creative community. Narratives espouse ideals, offer models for conduct, and register grievances. Myths can draw our focus away from history and into an imaginative mirage, or they can point the way to a more historical or complicated past. While some mythmaking activity is slight—perhaps a modest joke of little importance or a story about one's morning activities—other mythmaking activities may result in the institution of pervasive and systematic values of exclusion and hierarchy.

In the section on "narratives about evil," we discussed how myth-making makes use of a stylized presentation of material to foster bonds of solidarity and create a common enemy. In these relatively simple stories, certain kinds of behavior are shunned while others exalted. In the section on stories of sacrifice and womanhood, we see a form of storytelling that recommends appropriate conduct for a wife and mother, as well as cautions for those who might contradict these ideals. Lastly, in the section on androcentrism, we see a widespread network of male-centered myths recapitulated across several domains that promote the exclusion of women from the historical and scientific record. In all three examples, there are clear recommendations about what is and isn't dangerous. Dangers and aversions populate every aspect of the myths we've examined. The power of myth is an extension of its creative employment of magical systems of classification and the expectations it fosters regarding acceptable forms of interaction. Myths facilitate the ranking of essences as well as the ritualization of interactions between members and groups. As scholars of mythmaking, our aim is twofold: (1) to better understand how myths are created, maintained, and transformed and (2) to examine how myths make use of the materials at hand to direct our attention, focus our gaze, and order our priorities.

As we've seen, mythmaking is a design strategy for advancing interests. In addition to manipulating bonds of solidarity, mythmaking also recalibrates classification systems, hierarchies, and rankings. In short, it is an ideal vehicle for articulating and registering dangers and aversions. One of the magical characteristics of mythmaking is its power of apophenia. Apophenia is a term used to describe how random elements are connected to one another in meaningful ways.[62] Ritual can't do this. Rituals can create tighter bonds of solidarity, but because of their impoverished capacity to refer to reality, they can't do the connective work of linking people, events, and places. Mythmaking, on the other hand, is ideal for this task. Storytelling allows us to establish meaningful associations between distant or unrelated things. The rose comes to signify passion, the corpse handler signifies death pollution. The death of a husband, mythically defined as premature, becomes a sign of an impious wife, at least until she commits herself to the flames or can counter the myth with another myth of greater obligation to family. But it isn't just magical association that makes myth powerful. Mythmaking also makes use of another piece of our dangers and aversions puzzle: strong emotions. Without affect, our myths may fall to pieces.

---

62. Susan Lepselter, *The Resonance of Unseen Things: Poetics, Power, Captivity, and UFOs in the American Uncanny* (Ann Arbor, MI: University of Michigan Press, 2016), 3–5.

Chapter 5

Strong Emotions

Strong emotions are important constituents of our attitudes and practices concerning dangers and aversions. While anger, fear, happiness, and sadness are often at the top of the list of the big human emotions, I've selected shame and disgust as exemplary aversive emotions. When we experience shame, we want to disappear. Shame presents us with a profoundly unsettling experience and a desire to avoid the gaze of others. When we experience disgust, we want the offending object to disappear. Disgust inspires a revulsion and aversion and a desire to cleanse. While the particular aversions of shame and disgust vary from context to context, each emotion exhibits a high degree of similarity across cultures. For example, what people find disgusting varies, but we find disgust almost everywhere. In addition to being aversive emotions, shame and disgust express to others a strong sense of danger. Objects deemed disgusting are rejected, and there is a strong desire not to be associated with them. The prospect of social rejection is also dangerous, striking at our very sense of self in relation to others. Both of these emotions, although in very different ways, play a significant part in our dealings with others and in our dealings with objects.

Emotions operate in tandem with culture, and so we would expect context to play an overriding role in our expression and recognition of these emotions. As much as emotions serve as vehicles of culture, they also work on culture. Like language, emotions are mediums of apprehension and representations for our cognitions. We think with emotions, and we think about emotions. Despite the widespread notion that emotions are relatively private, I follow Philippe Rochat, who conceptualizes emotions as having a primarily communicative function. Emotions are behavioral expressions linked to our feelings and affects and are, in principle, readable by others.[1] It is the legibility of emotions that allows them to be performed without being felt, whether in the theatre or on the street. Unlike the previous chapters which house a key category and three examples, this chapter has four main sections. I will outline two distinct emotions with a single example for each.

Shame and Self-Knowledge

Although there is a vast literature on emotions and affects, I prefer Rochat's work because it so thoroughly grasps the idea that emotions are social.[2] The human psyche, Rochat writes, "is primarily determined by the pervasive propensity to have others in mind."[3] Despite the sociality of our emotional lives, shame is surprisingly not often identified as one of the big or obvious emotions.[4] We all experience shame, and it very likely constitutes one of the core features of self-consciousness. As Rochat notes, "shame is a central emotion, the epitome of self-consciousness," and the concept captures "a profound, complex, and too often neglected emotion: the experience of self in relation to others."[5] Shame encompasses the internalization of first and third-person perspectives, perspectives first encountered in our earliest interactions with others.

---

1. "Feelings stand for the perception of what is experienced from within namely, moods and fluctuating affective climates, which oscillate between elation and depression, intense pleasure and pain. Affects stand for constantly changing distinct internal climates or moods that are perceived via feelings." Philippe Rochat, "Shame and Self-Knowledge," *Others in Mind: Social Origins of Self-Consciousness* (Cambridge: Cambridge University Press 2009), 111.

2. Rochat, "Shame and Self-Knowledge," 105–117.

3. Rochat, "Shame and Self-Knowledge," 105.

4. Martha C. Nussbaum's *Hiding from Humanity: Disgust, Shame, and the Law* (Princeton, NJ: Princeton University Press, 2004) is a notable exception.

5. Rochat, "Shame and Self-Knowledge," 105.

When discussing shame in class, I often start by asking students about strategies that professors use to shame them.[6] Students are remarkably quick in identifying a range of shaming strategies. Some of these strategies strike me as embarrassing (calling on a student who has fallen asleep in class) or as constructive (providing feedback on a poorly written essay). Others are simply cruel or racist: mocking something a student says in response to a question or deriding a student for belonging to a particular ethnic group or community.[7] Then I turn the tables and ask students how they shame their professors. The responses also vary from the embarrassing (you've spilled something on your clothing; you use too many big words) to the cruel (posting misogynist comments about a female professor online).[8]

While shaming can be strategic, shame begins with our need for affiliation and a sense of belonging, as well as our fear of being rejected. The concept of shame encompasses the negative connotation of knowledge of the self in relation to other—a gap that can be experienced as painful and, at times, a gap that inspires a degree of generalized disturbance. Freezing at the sight of oneself in a polished surface, watching oneself speak in a Zoom meeting, or boisterously clowning in front of a mirror are all examples of this disturbance. The well documented anxiety people experience when faced with

---

6. Inspired by Paul A. Trout, "Shame on You," *CAUT Bulletin* (December 2006), retrieved June 25, 2021, from https://bulletin-archives.caut.ca/bulletin/articles/2006/12/shame-on-you.

7. For a study of racism in the classroom, see Sheila Cote-Meek, *Colonized Classrooms: Racism, Trauma and Resistance in Post-Secondary Education* (Winnipeg: Fernwood Publishing, 2014). Racism in the classroom was one of the sections of the Indigenizing Curriculum Summer Institute (University of Manitoba, 2018). Three Indigenous students spoke about their experiences of racism at the University of Manitoba—racism from professors, peers, and administrators. McCallum and Perry refer to these experiences as "the Indigenous everyday." McCallum and Perry, *Structures of Indifference*, 7.

8. If I can add a bit of a sidenote, shame is an everyday and ordinary experience. Whenever I've raised these examples in class, students often extend the conversation by talking about how they've shamed or been shamed by a sibling. I will simply observe that, as a society, we've become exceptionally skilled at hurting one another.

speaking in public is another example. As Rochat suggests, "Public speech is bread and butter not only for teachers, lawyers, writers, or people in academia, but also for the growing number of people working in the corporate world. On the job, people are increasingly put on stage, and, more often than not, they hate it."[9]

Rochat's essay on shame draws our attention to the remarkable discrepancy between first-person and third-party perspectives. When we are on stage, our slips of speech, mumbles, or missed words are easily forgotten and forgiven by most audiences. But it rarely feels this way. Small mishaps scarcely noticed by an audience may throw us into despair. I've left countless lectures wrangling over a poorly chosen illustration or careless phrasing of a point. This gap between actor and spectator forms the core issue of self-consciousness and an emotion central to our sense of self: shame.

Anxieties and fears about public speaking, to keep with the example provided by Rochat, may be the result of a culture that prizes individualism and professional comportment. Still, while the specifics may vary, there is merit to Rochat's claim that shame will be our constant companion so long as we have others in mind. To use another anecdotal example, when discussing this essay during my most recent Evil class, I asked by way of a show of hands if students would be comfortable coming to the front of the class to explain some of what they'd just read. I further asked them to visualize doing so. In a class composed of over 150 students, only a handful of hands were raised. More prevalent than raised hands was the visible appearance of near-panic across the room. The gap between what we perceive as self-presentation and what one thinks is perceived by others "forms the core issue of self-consciousness."[10] In Rochat's view, the anxiety is the expression of the basic affiliation need and its corollary, the fear of isolation or separation from others.[11]

Rochat's second example concerns a beggar on the street near where he lives. The beggar "is sitting on the sidewalk with an empty yogurt box in front of him, his head down, always holding the same

9. Rochat, "Shame and Self-Knowledge," 107.

10. Rochat, "Shame and Self-Knowledge," 109.

11. Rochat, "Shame and Self-Knowledge," 109

torn cardboard sign on it, a shaky, handwritten message that reads, in fading blue ink, 'Jobless and hungry.'"[12] Rochat observes that, in passing the beggar, we are drawn into the orbit of social rejection. We can ignore the beggar or sympathize. Whether faked or not, the beggar's shame is carefully displayed and performed in a staging to which we can all relate. Rochat describes the performance as follows:

> The self-display by this man connotes that he is an honest worker who lost his job and has to beg as a last resort to feed himself and maybe his family. Collapsed on the sidewalk, head down as a sign of resignation, avoiding the fast passing gazes that might fall upon him, the man is exquisitely staging his misery and humiliation. His self-presentation forces us to empathize and eventually act upon his experience of social rejection by dropping a coin or two into his cup.[13]

The staging of rejection and attendant shame is intended to have communicative impact. As Rochat puts it, the performance displays the tragedy of being left out: "the feeling of being pushed out from the protective enclosure of others."[14] Shame expresses this feeling of rejection and lack of recognition, arising from "the comparison and devaluation of the self in relation to others and their judging eyes."[15] Shame is the communicable expression of the feelings and affects associated with social rejection: "in its prototypical expression, it is avoidant in the sense of a general propensity to *hide* away and *flee* from public scrutiny."[16] Unlike many of the other emotions, which can be experienced with a degree of pleasure (pain, hate, anger), shame affords no such comfort: "No one enjoys being socially rejected—no one."[17] "Shame *is the avoidant behavioral expression of being exposed to public scrutiny.* Evidently, behind such expression lies the fear of being judged, hence disowned and ultimately rejected by others."[18]

---

12. Rochat, "Shame and Self-Knowledge," 110.
13. Rochat, "Shame and Self-Knowledge," 110.
14. Rochat, "Shame and Self-Knowledge," 110.
15. Rochat, "Shame and Self-Knowledge," 111.
16. Rochat, "Shame and Self-Knowledge," 112.
17. Rochat, "Shame and Self-Knowledge," 113.
18. Rochat, "Shame and Self-Knowledge," 113.

As part of a communicative system, the emotion need not necessarily be felt in order to trigger a response. The staging of shame can be rooted in the performance of a commonly accepted expressive culture. Local cultures have their own idioms for communicating and understanding expressions of rejection. Performing and witnessing the feelings and affects of social rejection elicits our sense of self in relation to others in a rather unavoidable way. As Rochat makes the point over and over, we have others in mind.

Rochat further notes that oppositional forms of expression derive in part from shame. These forms of expression and posturing are "behaviour buffers against social rejection."[19] Contempt, hubris, and pride are self-conscious emotions rooted in our anxieties about rejection. Contempt and pride are more proactive expressions of superiority and form a shield against social judgement, providing self-assurance in the face of others.[20] These emotions put distance and estrangement between self and other: "Contempt turns social rejection the other way around: now it is the self that rejects others."[21]

Empathy works not by means of rejection but by means of fusion—the closing of the distance between self and other. When we empathize, we project feelings from third to first person. As Rochat suggests, "We perceive and can relate to what others are perceiving of their own mood and affects from within the privacy of their own bodies."[22] Empathy emerges out of a generalized fear of social rejection. Like pride and contempt, empathy regulates painful feelings. A coin is dropped in the cup of the beggar out of empathy, or the beggar can be ignored out of contempt. In both instances, we are negotiating with the basic fear of rejection and are brought into the orbit of shame.

---

19. Rochat, "Shame and Self-Knowledge," 114.

20. Robin De'Angelo's *White Fragility* (Boston, MA: Beacon Press, 2018) is a tangible example. When read alongside Rochat we see that white fragility is rooted in shame and describes how white people negotiate racism: tears of empathy or the distancing of contempt and supremacy.

21. Rochat, "Shame and Self-Knowledge," 114.

22. Rochat, "Shame and Self-Knowledge," 114.

In a more expansive sense, the experience of shame runs a fairly wide spectrum. From the blush of embarrassment to paralyzing fear of judgement and condemnation, our need for recognition and affiliation with others is a constitutive element of human self-consciousness. While acceptable or recognized expressions of shame are shaped by local cultures, the experience of co-consciousness is an integral part of our shared sense of self/other. Cognition and communication have their roots in human culture, but these aspects of culture have elements that are prevalent throughout human history and experience. Shame is rooted in socially constituted cognition, or the dynamics of multiple perspectives and attachments.

Example: Honour and Shame

"Seeds of Honor, Fields of Shame" is an essay by Carol Delaney about sexuality and procreation in a small village about 80 kilometers from Ankara, Turkey.[23] Based on fieldwork from 1980–1982, Delaney explores notions of honor and shame in the context of gender and sexuality among people who considered themselves to be "true Anatolian Turks and professed to be Sunni, rather than Alevi, Muslims."[24] While I do not think it is possible to map the actual emotional context of shame within the village, I think we can use what we have learned about shame and self-knowledge to speculate on the affective power of shame and its derivatives to shape and maintain social norms and practices concerning gender and sexuality.

For Rochat, shame concerns the painful discrepancy between perceptions of the self and imagined perceptions of others. For Delaney, however, shame refers to the "genetic coding" or structure of relations generative of possibilities.[25] She's not using shame to describe an emotive expression. In the context of sexuality, gender, and

---

23. Carol Delaney, "Seeds of Honor, Fields of Shame," in David Gilmore, ed., *Honor and Shame and the Unity of the Mediterranean* (Washington, DC: American Anthropological Association, 1987), 35–48.

24. Delaney, *The Seed and Soil*, 21.

25. Delaney, "Seeds of Honor," 35.

procreation in this village, honor is a primary attribute of men, and shame is a primary attribute of women. Honor and shame are part of a system of expectations about behavior. Delaney explains this in terms of ideas about how life comes into being and about the construction, perception, and context of procreation. Honor and shame are functions of a specific construction and entwinement of procreation and monotheism.[26]

Delaney begins by mentioning that honor and shame are familiar concepts and caught up in a very old but ongoing discussion within the discipline of anthropology about the distinctiveness of Mediterranean societies. However, we can use what we know of the emotion shame to explore and speculate about the ambience of self-consciousness and the fear of rejection within the village. More than this, looking at shame as an emotion helps us understand the rich and complex strategies of borderwork—practices designed to assure affiliation and stave off rejection.

According to the narratives of Turkish villagers shared with Delaney, gender is defined by the role one has in procreation: the role of a male is to plant the seed and the role of a female is to bring it forth.[27] Delaney indicates that women are objectified in this view. Villagers occasionally cite the Qu'ran to support this view: "Women are given to you as fields, go therein and sow your seed."[28] "The female body, like soil, is a generalized medium of nurture," serving as a vessel for the seed and engendering all aspects of the essential identity. Delaney calls this conception of procreation "monogenetic." The cultivated soil is an enclosed field, covered or owned by a man who earns honor by being able to guarantee that his field has been properly enclosed, thus securing his seed in particular.[29]

---

26. Delaney, "Seeds of Honor," 36.

27. For an alternative view of sex and reproduction, see Nahyan Fancy, "Generation in Medieval Islamic Medicine," in Nick Hopwood, Rebecca Flemming, and Lauren Kassell, eds., *Reproduction: Antiquity to the Present Day* (Cambridge: Cambridge University Press, 2018), 129–140. Thanks to Lisa Alexandrin for this reference.

28. Sura 2 223 cited in Delaney, "Seeds of Honor," 38.

29. Delaney, "Seeds of Honor," 38–39.

In this conception of procreation, "it is men who give the life, women merely give birth."[30] Life instantiated by the seed is eternal. As Delaney notes, "A boy is the flame of the line, a girl is the embers of a house."[31] If a man has no sons, his hearth has extinguished: "It is a fate worse than death."[32] The generativity of the seed reflects and is reflected in monotheism, the practice of male circumcision, and the pride associated with "full membership in the brotherhood of Islam."[33] The penis is "explicitly denoted as the ticket of admission to the realm of the sacred."[34]

The association of maleness and the sacred leaves femaleness to be associated with the profane or, as Delaney puts it, the "indiscriminate."[35] While the social perception of village men to engender identity serves as the foundation of their honor, this foundation is prone to an extreme anxiety about the legitimacy of a child. Men's honor is easily shaken by the behavior of women. The field metaphor is not literal but has extended application. Like real fields, women are to be enclosed. This borderwork is applied not only to women but also to the village as a whole since the village and the community is coded as female. A man secures his seed by ensuring that his wife is properly enclosed or covered, just as the village secures their property by ensuring that the borders are properly enclosed through arranged marriages. Tremendous effort is devoted to organizing village life in a way that protects a man's honor. When social norms concerning gender and sexuality are at work, everyday interactions become a minefield of dangers and aversions.

Delaney describes a stark contrast between construals of masculinity and femininity, "Women, on the contrary, are, by their created nature, already ashamed, the recognition of their constitutional inferiority constitutes the feeling of shame. Shame is an inevitable part of being female, a woman is honorable if she remains cognizant of

---

30. Delaney, "Seeds of Honor," 39.
31. Delaney, "Seeds of Honor," 39.
32. Delaney, "Seeds of Honor," 39.
33. Delaney, "Seeds of Honor," 39.
34. Delaney, "Seeds of Honor," 39.
35. Delaney, "Seeds of Honor," 41.

this fact and its implications for behavior, and she is shameless if she forgets."[36] This dynamic is reinforced by stories of Eve's act of disobedience, which is thought to have brought literal dirtiness into the world: urination, sweating, and defecation. The men of the village also speak of menstruation as signifying female impurity.[37] Shame is attributed to women because of her "indiscriminate fecundity" that can be redeemed only by constraint.[38] From the perspective of men in the village, women lack both agency and an identity rooted in the eternal. Male villagers often view women as having an indiscriminate dispositions as being unable to exercise choice. A field is open to anyone, which is why it must be fenced.

The matrix of gender, sex, and procreation is ripe with fears of ostracism—with dangers and aversions. The possibility of rejection is a constant structural feature of village life. The village in question has a history of excluding outsiders. As a buffer against this, masculinity is structured along the lines of pride—a pre-emptive social distancing from others, especially women. The eclipse of women's agency in the eyes of men allows men to ignore the gap between first- and third-person perspective. Men who deny women's agency don't have to confront the possibility of contradiction, although they must still feverishly manage their fences and fields.

Delaney discusses shame more as an organizational principle than an affect, although she makes clear that shame is caught up in feelings, experiences, and systems of meaning. When Rochat speaks about shame, he's talking about our anxieties concerning social rejection. Any aspect of identity can be a source of rejection. In the village discussed by Delaney, all aspects of identity are on display, and there are any number of ways in which even a small or minor deviations from expectations may solicit either empathy or contempt.

Self-knowledge, self-consciousness, and meticulous attention to detail are hallmark features of our anxieties about affiliation and rejection. Everything must be staged just right and must send the

---

36. Delaney, "Seeds of Honor," 40.

37. Contrarily, as Delaney notes, women see menstruation as a cleansing process. Delaney, "Seeds of Honor," 40.

38. Delaney, "Seeds of Honor," 40.

right communicative signals. When relations within a community are highly ritualized, the risk of impurity (social rejection) will be a constant feature. Drawing shame into the circle of Rochat's understanding of emotions helps us see how powerful affects influence our senses, narratives (myths), and performances (rituals). A formal consideration of shame also helps us see how vigilance about the body—its placement and comportment—can become the object of such care and attention.

Shame is accompanied by aversions, fears, and anxieties. When the body and the body politic are imagined together, anxieties about the rejected body will be refracted unevenly into anxieties about political and social bodies. Shame is, as Rochat argues, the epitome of a self-consciousness that is inescapably as political as it is social. While Delaney speaks of shame as a gendered phenomenon, with shame as an attribute of women and honor an attribute of men, Rochat's conception of shame grasps a crucial feature of human social ecology. For Delaney, shame anxieties result from a system of norms, contributing to gendered divisions and compulsive concerns with boundary crossing. For Rochat, however, shame is an attribute of everyone and manifests in any number of ways. Shame coaxes behavior into conformity with expectations about gender performance, whether in the service of preserving male authority and creating spaces for separate female solidarity or in the service of social distancing from others by means of pride and exclusion. It is Rochat's rendering of shame that we employ here in our consideration of dangers and aversions. Anxieties about rejection that accompany shame compel contextually specific behavior, prompting cooperation and sponsoring authorizing discourses which might otherwise meet with criticism or revolt.

With this in mind, the specific context of Delaney's account should not be treated as accidental. Her larger work, *The Seed and Soil*, explains how the metaphors used in the village bind a wide range of elements together: bodies, land, food, marriage, relationships, and authority. The symbols that make these creative linkages reflect attitudes towards not only procreation and divinity but also land and placement. We should also resist the temptation to use what we know about the emotional power of shame to explain sex and gender relations in the historical context of Delaney's ethnographic account of a

Turkish village. What we can do, however, is think about how shame works to bolster and reinforce social norms. The affective power of shame prompts us to seek affiliation and avoid rejection, and it operates as a formidable force in weaving together disparate groups. Women are able to bond and affiliate as women (daughters, wives, mothers) just as men are able to take pride in their shared manhood.

Thus, affiliation and aversion are inextricably linked. Aversion to the painful experience of shame may lead men to create an enclave of male pride, a pre-emptive social distancing from others. The normative shaming of women as a group also creates female solidarity, networks of affiliation and acceptance (and counter-narrative). Given its power and volatility, systems of shame curate extensive awareness of "purity and danger." Anxieties about being unrecognized or rejected provide powerful motivations to shape communities of exclusion and strong emotional affiliation. In other words, shame and other strong emotions are tools of social formation. The key point here is that dangers and aversions shape how the self is perceived in relation to others. This tension is never relaxed. Therefore, social formations generated by self-consciousness help us see a range of dangers and aversions that might otherwise go unnoticed.

Disgust: Revulsion and Aversion

Disgust is pretty much a role model emotion for dangers and aversions. Disgust is theorized as a rejection response that developed to protect the body from poisons and contamination. As the response evolved, it migrated from serving as a mechanism guarding the mouth and body from harm to a being a gatekeeper of the soul.[39] Unlike the wealth of research on fear, anger, happiness, and sadness,

---

39. P. Rozin, J. Haidt, and C. R. McCauley, "Disgust," in M. Lewis, J. M. Haviland-Jones, and L. Feldman Barrett, eds., *Handbook of Emotions*, 3rd edition (New York: Guilford Press, 2008), 757. Note—this understanding of disgust remains contested. Anxieties about oral incorporation may be one of several possible starting points for disgust. The potency of disgust and its usefulness for social formation is unchanged regardless of the origin story.

disgust received scant attention until the 1990s. Many basic questions about disgust—concerning its origins, development, or even its status as an emotion—are still unanswered. However, even though what elicits disgust is determined by the details of a particular culture, the "face of disgust" and its aversive qualities (rejection and revulsion) appear to be highly cross-cultural. Unlike other emotions like shame, disgust appears to be rather limited in duration, with its affective characteristics disappearing when offending elicitors are removed or put out of mind.

According to Rozin, Haidt, and McCauley, disgust is rooted in what they characterize as "core disgust." Core disgust is one of several categories of food rejection (along with distaste, danger, and inappropriateness). Unlike distaste, which is triggered by sensory perceptions, disgust is primarily ideational. Disgust is often rooted in what we think about the nature or origin of potential food. There was no shortage of buzz when stories circulated that "the world's most expensive coffee" is produced by passing through the digestive system of the civet or that artificial vanilla can be produced using a beaver's anal excretions.[40]

Rozin and his collaborators argue that an appraisal eliciting core disgust requires a sense of potential oral incorporation, offensiveness, and contamination potency.[41] When taken together, these appraisals are not only expressions of aversion to potential diseases and toxins but also key elements of collective identity. As discussed in the section on magical thinking, there is a tendency to assume that we are what we eat. Concepts of pollution and contamination are very much tied up in our disgust response and our implicit assumptions about self, other, and incorporation.

---

40. Mollie Bloudoff-Indelicato, "Beaver Butts Emit Goo used for Vanilla Flavoring," *National Geographic* (October 1, 2013), retrieved June 25, 2021, from www.nationalgeographic.com/animals/article/beaver-butt-goo-vanilla-flavoring. Rachael Bale, "The Disturbing Secret Behind the World's Most Expensive Coffee," National Geographic (April 29, 2016), retrieved June 25, 2021, from www.nationalgeographic.com/animals/article/160429-kopi-luwak-captive-civet-coffee-Indonesia.

41. Rozin, Haidt, McCauley, "Disgust," 759.

Aversion to aspects of animal nature are fairly widespread and can be further divided into four domains: inappropriate sexual acts, poor hygiene, death, and violations of the bodily envelope. While all four of these domains involve potential sources of biological contagion and infection, Rozin, Haidt, and McCauley suggest that there is more going on here than appears. Cultures prescribe proper ways to handle corpses, have sex, or wash. The disgust response is triggered not simply by a concern for disease but, importantly, by the norms and prohibitions that have accrued around certain forms of contact or interaction. This is even more pronounced when it comes to interpersonal disgust, which "clearly discourages contact with other human beings who are not intimates" and moral disgust, which includes a particular class of judgements centering around purity of the body and soul.[42]

Given the remarkable range of disgust elicitors, identifying objects of universal aversion is difficult, if not impossible. However, the emotion disgust exhibits a high degree of cross-cultural expression. While what we find disgusting is local, that we find things disgusting in the first place is not. Disgust requires enculturation and, like shame, is thoroughly social. Disgust may be acquired or learned by witnessing facial displays and aversion behavior. It also requires a fair degree of imagination. Rozin, Haidt, and McCauley note that, in most instances, adult contamination sensitivity is a mixture of at least two types of conceptions: the transfer of invisible material through contact and a more indelible "spiritual" force that is not subject to removal by chemical and physical treatments.[43] While dealing with invisible entities is identifiable in early childhood, the coding of invisible entities as dangerous requires a fair bit of cultural work.[44] Thinking about disgust in the context of evil (dangers and aversions) helps us see some of the more subtle partners of moral judgement.

---

42. Rozin, Haidt, McCauley, "Disgust," 761–763.
43. Rozin, Haidt, McCauley, "Disgust," 765.
44. Rozin, Haidt, McCauley, "Disgust," 765.

Example: Disgust and Enlightenment

The first chapter of *Charming Cadavers* by Liz Wilson provides an excellent illustration of how strong emotions serve projects of social formation.[45] Wilson's chapter "Celibacy and the Social World" discusses the strategies used by Buddhist renouncers to achieve the "aha experience" of enlightenment.[46] Wilson notes that Indian Buddhist hagiography is filled with scenes of transformation "in which worldly, dissatisfied renouncers—especially lovesick monks and vain nuns—become serious, committed renouncers when they suddenly perceive the truth of the Dharma or cosmic order displayed in the world."[47] Such shocks of recognition can be brought about by the sight of beautiful things, like the body of the Buddha, or of things that incite pity and convey impermanence or suffering, like sickness.

Of particular interest here are stories of the shock of recognition brought about in the charnel fields. The charnel fields are repositories of corpses, some having been abandoned by the community due to the cost of wood and oil for cremation. Several of the "aha experiences" described in post-Aśokan hagiographies occur through the practicing of a technique known as meditation on foulness, a technique praised by the Buddha of the Pāli canon and detailed in the writings of the fifth century commentator Buddhaghosa. It is recommended that the meditator contemplate corpses in various stages of decay, with an emphasis on the stage of decay that most corresponds with their desires and attachments. Furthermore, it is written that the cultivation of a sense of foulness, achieved by meditating on a corpse, may serve as an antidote to desire. As much as meditation on foulness is recommended, a small cautionary note is provided: the corpse should be the same sex as the meditator, lest the latter be overtaken by irresistible sexual desire. Nevertheless, navigating around the cautions of recorded wisdom, it appears that many monks

---

45. Liz Wilson, "Celibacy and the Social World," *Charming Cadavers: Horrific Figurations of the Feminine in Indian Buddhist Hagiographic Literature* (Chicago, IL: University of Chicago Press, 1996), 15–39.

46. Wilson, "Celibacy and the Social World," 15.

47. Wilson, "Celibacy and the Social World," 15.

did not heed Buddhaghosa's (heteronormative) warning: "Stories in which prominent monks contemplate dead women with salutary results at watershed moments in their monastic careers appear quite frequently."[48]

Vividly portrayed here are "horrific figurations of the feminine" to incite masculine enlightenment by means of disgust. Rozin and colleagues argue that core disgust is rooted in the prospect of merging: you are what you eat, but you are also what you affiliate with. Consumption, sex, and kinship are all forms of fusion, which is why disgust is an interesting mechanism of disaffiliation. As mentioned earlier, the core experience of food aversions easily migrates into other domains and is leveraged through the cultural association of femininity with a conception of impermanence. Death, decay, violations of the body are all common elicitors of disgust and are all at the forefront of the practice's staging. But we also see that femininity is rapidly folded into the practice and equally associated with death and decay by means of narrative (mythmaking).

> Hagiographies that climax in horrific figurations of the feminine are extremely graphic; they assault the senses like an open wound. The reader or listener cannot help but recoil from the stark images of decaying beauty these stories present. Through this visceral experience of revulsion, one can achieve an existential awareness of the first Noble Truth (Pāli, *ariya-sacca*; Sanskrit, *arya-satya*) of Buddhism: the dis-ease or dissatisfaction that dogs even the most pleasurable of sensations.[49]

Binding femininity with death and decay allows these hagiographies to articulate re-descriptions of social life as something to be experienced as revolting. As Wilson notes, the Buddha of the Pāli canon frequently recommends avoiding women altogether. While this is done in the name of sexual desire, the overriding lesson has to do with our emotional response to the foulness within the body and the manipulation of the plasticity of disgust in order to augment tensions between the monastic community and the realm of householders.

---

48. Wilson, "Celibacy and the Social World," 16.
49. Wilson, "Celibacy and the Social World," 17.

The tenacity and unique characteristics of disgust readily serve as an excellent vehicle for this task. Leveraging disgust by means of narrative allows the monastic community to re-describe the social life of the *Sangha* as free and pure and the social life of the family as claustrophobia-producing: "an oppressively close place such as the vagina or womb... extremely tight and disgustingly impure."[50]

Along with its relatively short duration, disgust's malleability and its ability to cross from one domain into another make it amenable to any number of manipulations. If taken seriously, the redescription of home life as a kind of quagmire should prompt householders to experience domestic life not as one of affiliation and community but as impure and disgusting—as a place of potential chaos. The power of myth to trigger this kind of radical upheaval and the power of an emotion to make the myth palpable suggest that strong emotions are key players in solidifying identifications of dangers and aversions.

Conclusion

Strong emotions play a foundational role in attachments, dangers, and aversions. Shame and disgust are a couple of the more noteworthy emotions that move people to cleanse and purify or avoid and reject. Despite the ubiquity of disgust, what we find disgusting is intricately woven into the specific fabrics of culture, where we cannot expect to find universals. Disgust and shame are highly malleable aspects of encultured cognition. Emotions are strong attractors or repellents, and they contribute to what people want and do not want in their lives. They don't work in isolation, however. Emotions are deeply embedded in culture and are part of the social tapestry of discourses identified through this book as classification, ritual, and myth.

When we classify, we create boundaries and a sense of what is in and what is out. These are highly social activities because classification systems govern norms as much as they do facts. Classification schemas are maintained and reworked by means of mythmaking and

---

50. Wilson, "Celibacy and the Social World," 28.

buttressed by the interdependent workings of magical thinking, rituals, and emotions. Myths make use of symbols, and magical thinking contributes to our sense of disgust as much as shame contributes to our mythmaking. These pieces are interlaced, but each sheds light on a different question and a different kind of relationship. However, in this experiment there is still one more piece in our puzzle—a piece that is designed quite specifically to register and chart dangers and aversions: morality.

Chapter 6

Morality

Unlike many of the other elements that contribute to our sense of dangers and aversions integrally but indirectly, morality begins with dangers and aversions as its focus. Morality is a discourse through which dangers and aversions are refined and clarified. From the initial experience of indignation to the process of holding one another accountable for our actions, morality articulates our sense of transgression and violation, as well as our capacities for social solidarity and human agency. Moral discourse creates and recommends a procedure for identifying dangers and aversions with an emphasis on rights, agency, autonomy, and solidarity. Curiously, moral discourse also provides a critique of the coercive influences of magical thinking, ritual, myth, and strong emotions when assessing and dealing with dangers and aversions in a deliberative context. In many respects, morality articulates a form of social solidarity that aims to dismantle the authorizations created by the previously mentioned categories.

In common usage, morality refers to a sense of right and wrong. The concept as used here maintains that connotation but does so with reference to the process in which such judgements are made. A deliberative conception of morality proposes an impartial procedure for resolving questions of right and wrong. The decision-making process is not separate from the conclusion. A deliberative conception of morality, as outlined within communications theory, refers to the process of adjudicating norms as much as it refers to the norms themselves.[1]

---

1. See Jürgen Habermas's "Discourse Ethics: Notes on a Program of Philosophical Justification," *Moral Consciousness and Communicative Action*, trans. Christian Lenhardt and Shierry Weber Nicholsen (Cambridge, MA: MIT Press, 1990), 43–115. To be clear, I am using the term morality here to refer to

A deliberative conception of morality emphasizes communication free from coercion. "Harm" is defined within moral philosophy as that which interferes with or compromises agency, solidarity, and human dignity. Mythmaking and ritual are, from a moral point of view, social forces that exert ideological power. Morality encompasses a deliberative process critical of ideological and coercive expressions of power and authority, aiming to replace them with what Jürgen Habermas calls "communicative power"—the power of cooperative, reasonable, and non-violent decision-making. Morality is constituted by our capacity to understand one another and persuade one another of the soundness of norms through the public use of reason. In this way, morality is explicitly dissociated from the affective influences of magical thinking, ritual, myth, and strong emotions.

In *Discourse and the Construction of Society,* Bruce Lincoln outlines three discourses that contribute to social formation: myth, ritual, and classification. All make use of affects and constitute ideological forms of persuasion as opposed to brute force or physical coercion.[2] Morality, I think, forms another discourse involved in the construction of society. The difference is this: magical thinking, myth, and ritual are discourses that blend several forms of social interactions with instrumental success. In short, they form strategic discourses.[3] In Lincoln's conception, discourses are governed by a social interest that aims to bring about a specific state of affairs through

Habermas's deliberative conception of morality. Just as there are many theories of magical thinking, there are many theories of morality. I have adopted Habermas's conception of morality because it is the most interesting and productive for this project. I should emphasize that it is used here as a key category. This chapter is not a moralizing bookend. Morality is used redescriptively to refer to the interesting way in which we make decisions about dangers and aversions.

2. Lincoln, *Discourse and the Construction of Society.*

3. Strategic discourses combine instrumental and communicative forms of reasoning. If a group of people plot to steal money from a bank, the group will coordinate their activities consensually even if breaking into the vault requires technical expertise that utilizes instrumental reason. Instrumental reason is governed by norms of success while communicative reason is governed by norms of mutual understanding and agreement. See Habermas, *The Theory of Communicative Action.*

physical force or ideological persuasion. In a complementary view, there is another kind of discourse that Habermas calls communicative. Communicative action is not oriented by success but by the attempt to understand something with someone. It is a discourse that works towards peaceable and consensual dealings with one another. Communicative reason takes the form of ideology critique when action situated in mutual understanding and agreement is compromised. Moral criticism aims to renew the possibility of deliberation free from the influence of coercive or ideological power.[4] Inspired by Habermas, this is the kind of discourse I am calling "moral."[5] This is how morality contrasts with the other key categories and why its conception of dangers and aversions is so precise.

In terms of dangers and aversions, moral conversations aim to provide classifications focusing on human dignity and norms that protect and promote human welfare. Human dignity is at the root of most discussions about human rights and responsibilities. Moral conversations identify practices that are dangerous or to be avoided by means of articulating how norms concerning right and wrong are generated, maintained, renewed, challenged, and discarded. These conversations are critical of social norms produced by the powers of magical thinking, mythmaking, ritualization, and strong emotions. We make a case for what is wrong not because it matches with our sense of disgust, because it coincides with a history of past classification or because it fits a bigger cosmic picture. Moral deliberations may include reference to all of these things, but right and wrong are determined not on the basis of conformity to the past or to gut reactions. Rather, people identify the categories of "right" and "wrong" on the basis of collective agreements in the present—adjudicating conflicting differences, interests, histories, and prejudices using a deliberative procedure. In this way, morality is a self-reflective

---

4. For an accessible overview and introduction to the normative foundations of critical theorizing, see Seyla Benhabib, *Critique, Norm, and Utopia* (New York: Columbia University Press, 1986).

5. Jürgen Habermas, *Moral Consciousness and Communicative Action*, and *Justification and Application: Remarks on Discourse Ethics*, trans. Ciaran Cronin (Cambridge, MA: MIT Press, 1994).

conversation about a group's motivations, collective interests, coordinated actions, and social obligations.

With its emphasis on norms and obligations, moral thinking helps make distinctions between different kinds of norms. We may feel a sense of outrage when someone places their muddy boots on the kitchen table, but is this outrage appropriate to the moral domain? Is it comparable to witnessing a catastrophe? Matter out of place may solicit disgust, but this perceived violation is adjudicated socially before being considered an affront to human dignity. Because moral discourse is practical, it is also humanizing. Moral discourse reverses the tide of depicting something or someone as an abomination. It is a discourse that encourages a working through of conflicting interpretations. What if the mud-walker provides a good reason or explanation for the transgression? "These aren't real boots, it's actually cake in the shape of dirty boots!" In the light of reasoned conversation, the outrage may evaporate. It may also be decided after some deliberation that, while muddy boots on the table constitutes a transgression of hygiene or etiquette, the violation falls short of a crime against humanity. Moral deliberations are conversations of collaboration and living together as much as they are about classification and discernment. Morality is attuned to making finer distinctions between norms of justice and non-generalizable matters of taste.

As mentioned in the Preface, I am not advocating for a moral theory of discourse here. I am using a Habermasian account of morality to help describe a discernable process of decision-making that aggressively aims to counteract ideas of danger and aversion that are rooted in unreflective forms of authorization.[6] While there are sev-

---

6. For another accessible account of morality relevant to this course of study I would recommend Hannah Arendt's *Eichmann in Jerusalem: A Report on the Banality of Evil* (New York: Penguin Classics, 2006). In Arendt's account of Eichmann's criminal trial, the accused is held to account not for what he did under duress, deception, or ignorance—but for what he did knowingly—willfully with intent. Had Eichmann been under the spell of ritualized authority or deceived about the nature of his contribution to mass murder his guilt would stand differently than it does. In Arendt's account, Eichmann is shown to know exactly what he is doing in his identification with the Nazi regime, its policies, motivations, and desired outcomes. For many years I used selections from Arendt's book in my teaching.

eral key essays on discourse ethics that could be used to explore the deliberative foundations of morality, I have found Jürgen Habermas's "The Concept of Human Dignity and the Realistic Utopia of Human Rights" to be a highly succinct and accessible starting point.[7] In this essay, Habermas identifies human dignity as the key ingredient of morality. As the source of our moral experiences, dignity expresses our intuitive sense of reciprocity as well as respect and registers transgressions and violations of the self.[8]

Habermas argues that, although the concept of human dignity was not thoroughly codified in national constitutions and international law until after the Second World War, the concept is central to the history and architecture of human rights.[9] Article 1 of the Universal Declaration of Human Rights begins with this statement: "All human beings are born free and equal in dignity and rights."[10] Human dignity refers to the respect and esteem of oneself and another that imparts the mutual recognition of equality and uniqueness, the universal humanity and the unique circumstances of an individual life. Violations of dignity are violations of respect and esteem, and they compromise the capacity of people to respond and hold others accountable. In Habermas's view, human dignity forms the basis of the egalitarian and universalistic substance of morality.[11]

---

7. Jürgen Habermas, "The Concept of Human Dignity and the Realistic Utopia of Human Rights," *The Crisis of the European Union*, trans. Ciaran Cronin (Malden, MA: Polity Press, 2012), 71–100.

8. See also Habermas's discussion of indignation in *Moral Consciousness and Communicative Action*, 45–47.

9. Habermas, "Concept of Human Dignity," 71.

10. Cited in Habermas, "Concept of Human Dignity," 71.

11. Those sympathetic to Habermas's understanding of morality use a variety of terms to describe the project. Other phrases include communicative ethics, discourse ethics, deliberative ethics as well as moral theory of discourse and deliberative morality. The centerpiece of discourse ethics is the notion that social norms are the result of deliberative processes. Morality refers to our propensity for respect and esteem as well as outrage when norms are violated. In a way, morality is both an idealizing compass about how things ought to be and a sensor for identifying violations. In addition to the works already cited, see Seyla Benhabib and Fred Dallmayr, eds., *The Communicative Ethics Controversy* (Cambridge, MA: MIT Press, 1990).

Habermas elaborates on the relation between dignity and rights with reference to the 2006 German Federal Constitutional Court's declaration that the "Aviation Security Act" enacted by the Bundestag was unconstitutional. The "Aviation Security Act" authorized the German armed forces to shoot down passenger aircraft which had been transformed into missiles in order to avert threats to an indeterminately large number of people on the ground (comparable to the attacks on the twin towers of the World Trade Center in the United States). The court decided that the killing of passengers by agencies of the state would be unconstitutional. The duty to protect the lives of potential victims of a terrorist attack, the court ruled, is secondary to the duty to respect human dignity of the passengers: "with their lives being disposed of unilaterally by the state, the persons on board the aircraft ... are denied the value which is due to a human being for his or her own sake."[12] People should be treated as ends in themselves and not merely as means to an end.

Habermas goes on to defend the position that discourses on human rights, which have consistently emerged as resistance to despotism, oppression and humiliation, have always been rooted in responses to violations of human dignity: "The appeal to human rights feeds off the outrage of the humiliated at the violation of their human dignity."[13] Far from a conceptual latecomer, Habermas argues that human dignity is the moral source from which all rights derive their substance.[14] He further outlines how human dignity grounds each of the basic categories of human rights. The classical package of human rights includes liberal rights and democratic rights of participation, securing basic economic and political freedoms. Habermas argues that these rights must be supplemented by social and cultural rights, guaranteeing individuals' "appropriate" share of the prosperity of a culture as a whole. He observes that, without constraints on increases in social inequality, it is not possible to prevent the exclusion of groups from social and cultural life. Human dignity, Habermas argues,

---

12. Cited in Habermas, "Concept of Human Dignity," 72.
13. Habermas, "Concept of Human Dignity," 75.
14. Habermas, "Concept of Human Dignity," 75.

"grounds the *indivisibility* of all categories of human rights."[15] It is not only the portal through which "the egalitarian and universalistic substance of morality is imported into law" but also the hinge which connects the morality of equal respect with democratic lawmaking.[16] The moral concept of human dignity serves as the source of our social obligation towards reciprocal recognition and the translation of these obligations into legal claims: "the legal recognition claimed by citizens reaches beyond the reciprocal moral recognition of responsible subjects; it has the concrete meaning of the respect demanded for a status that is deserved" and thus infused with a moral sense of dignity.[17]

It is helpful here to see not only the overlap but also the difference between moral obligations and legal demands. The tensions between moral and legal norms and between political promises and failures are inherent to a concept of morality that has an inventive aspect. The inventive aspect of morality—the registering and accounting of ongoing experiences of violation—appears whenever untenable social conditions emerge: the marginalization of impoverished social classes, the unequal treatment of women and men in the workplace, discrimination against cultural, linguistic, religious and racial minorities, and so on.[18] Thinking about the connection between human dignity, morality, and human rights is useful since it spells out in a rather obvious way the more critical function of morality as a seismic social register of particular kinds of dangers and aversions.

Two essays by Seyla Benhabib elaborate on the more critical aspects of morality. Her 1992 essay "The Generalized and the Concrete Other" is a critique of patriarchal and androcentric norms that limit the full participation of women in moral and political deliberations—showing how ideological forces work to exclude women's experiences. Benhabib helps us see how and why deliberative conceptions of morality expect moral conversations to be uncoupled from the essentializing characteristics of magical thinking, the auspices

---

15. Habermas, "Concept of Human Dignity," 80.
16. Habermas, "Concept of Human Dignity," 81.
17. Habermas, "Concept of Human Dignity," 86.
18. Habermas, "Concept of Human Dignity," 77.

of myth or ritual, and the more pathic affectations of strong emotions like disgust or shame. Her 2010 essay "The Return of Political Theology" on the "affair of the scarf" also provides a telling example of how democratic regimes compromise their moral intuitions by treating citizens as means to an end rather than with the respect and esteem to which moral discourse suggests they are entitled.[19] Dangers and aversions are seen in a twofold way here. First, we see the integrity of moral intuitions threatened by ideological influences relying on uncommunicative forms of social action. Second, morality identifies and registers dangers and aversions explicitly, recommending appropriate forms of conduct and charting undesirable outcomes.

Example 1: The Generalized and the Concrete Other

Benhabib asks the question: can there be a feminist contribution to moral philosophy? Her feminist analysis of moral philosophy is highly instructive because it identifies how and why women's experiences have been excluded from a field which purports to include everyone. Using the Kohlberg-Gilligan controversy as an example, Benhabib draws on moral insights articulated within feminist theory to reflectively critique ideological blind spots in moral philosophy.

The controversy in question involved Lawrence Kohlberg's proposal of a stage-based model of moral development and moral reasoning that emphasizes the moral maturation of individuals through stages (pre-conventional, conventional, post-conventional). Carol Gilligan and her co-workers observed several discrepancies in the findings of Kohlberg's model, such as regression from adulthood to adolescence and persistent lower stages of moral development for women when compared with their male peers. Gilligan and her co-workers

---

19. Seyla Benhabib, "The Generalized and the Concrete Other: The Kohlberg-Gilligan Controversy and Moral Theory," *Situating the Self: Gender, Community and Postmodernism in Contemporary Ethics* (New York: Routledge, 1992), 148–177; Seyla Benhabib, "The Return of Political Theology: The Scarf Affair in Comparative Constitutional Perspective in France, Germany, and Turkey," *Philosophy and Social Criticism* 36, no. 3–4 (2010), 451–471.

concluded that "Kohlbergian theory is valid only for measuring the development of one aspect of moral orientation, which focusses on justice and rights."[20] In order to address Kohlberg's anomalous findings, Murphy and Gilligan proposed a distinction between "postconventional formalism" and "postconventional contextualism." Postconventional formalism refers to a reasoning process of solving moral problems with concepts such as "the social contract" or "natural rights" (the perspective of the *generalized* other). Postconventional contextualism, on the other hand, refers to reasoning processes that show a propensity for empathy and sympathy for individuals (the perspective of the *particular* other). The distinction between the two orientations allowed Gilligan to recast conceptions of moral judgement, showing that "contextuality, narrativity and specificity" is not a sign of weakness but "a vision of moral maturity that views the self as a being immersed in a network of relationships with others."[21]

Making use of insights gathered from this controversy, Benhabib persists with her original question about the contribution of feminist theory to moral philosophy, outlining two premises of feminist theory. First, gender-sex systems are social-historical and symbolic constitutions of sexual difference and interpretations of anatomical differences. Gender-sex systems are grids through which "the self develops an *embodied* identity, a certain mode of being in one's body and of living the body." Second, "the historically known gender-sex systems have contributed to the oppression and exploitation of women."[22] Feminist theory responds to this by developing an explanatory-diagnostic analysis of women's oppression across history, culture and societies and by articulating an anticipatory-utopian critique of the norms and values of our current society and culture.[23] The first premise is social scientific, while the second is normative

---

20. Benhabib, "Generalized and the Concrete Other," 148.

21. Benhabib, "Generalized and the Concrete Other," 149. Benhabib does not weigh in on Gilligan's conclusions, which could be read to recommend a dual-track version of morality. Instead, Benhabib shows how Gilligan's insights can be used to articulate a critique of a one-sided conception of morality.

22. Benhabib, "Generalized and the Concrete Other," 152.

23. Benhabib, "Generalized and the Concrete Other," 152.

and philosophical. Benhabib's critique registers explicit resistance to the privatization and exclusion of women's experience from moral thinking. In what follows, I work through Benhabib's essay but do so somewhat re-descriptively, drawing on some of the key categories already discussed. I'm doing so to highlight the way in which morality is conceived primarily as a form of reasoned deliberation and ideology critique.

To explain how Kohlberg's theory ends up in such a contradictory space, Benhabib first observes that his working definition of morality is rooted in a conception that begins with Hobbes, a viewpoint that was articulated "in the wake of the dissolution of the Aristotelian-Christian world-view."[24] In ancient and medieval moral systems, human communities were situated and defined in relation to a larger and more encompassing conception of the good life.[25] In ancient and medieval thought, the proper moral place of a person was defined by actions appropriate to their station or placement within a hierarchy. This dynamic system, rife with dissent, criticism, and contradiction, became unhinged with the development of modern science, capitalist exchange, and the division of the social structure into various public and private spheres.[26] Thus, morality was uncoupled from a cosmological foundation and an all-encompassing vision of the good life. In this new founding, "justice alone becomes the center of moral theory when bourgeois individuals in a disenchanted universe face the task of creating the legitimate basis of the social order for themselves."[27] Our obligations to one another were said to be result from our interest in peace and prosperity or derived from moral norms. In both instances the good life is relegated to the private sphere and individual preference.[28] Kohlberg's understanding of morality is indebted to the Hobbesian break with all-encompassing cosmologies.

---

24. Benhabib, "Generalized and the Concrete Other," 154.
25. Benhabib, "Generalized and the Concrete Other," 154.
26. Benhabib, "Generalized and the Concrete Other," 154.
27. Benhabib, "Generalized and the Concrete Other," 154.
28. Benhabib, "Generalized and the Concrete Other," 154.

In this uncoupling of morality from the good life, a separation of public and private was invented and the domestic-familial realm of human activity (along with all things related to sex, nurturance, care, and reproduction) was swept outside of the domain of justice. The mythic architecture of this split can be detected in the "state of nature" metaphor. Benhabib cites Hobbes as offering us the clearest formulation: "Let us consider men ... as if but even now sprung out of the earth, and suddenly, like mushrooms, come to full maturity, without all kinds of engagement to each other."[29] The vision of Hobbes is one of absolute autonomy. Men are born and mature without mothers. "The state-of-nature metaphor provides a vision of the autonomous self: this is a narcissist who sees the world in his own image; who has no awareness of the limits of his own desires and passions; and who cannot see himself through the eyes of another."[30]

This particular mythmaking activity allows political philosophers to propagate an image of "man" that experiences difference as loss. The narcissistic wounds of "war, fear, domination, anxiety, and death" are dealt with by means of the social contract. The overthrown political patriarchy is replaced by a brotherhood of equals and, in this process, the fraternity turns its attention "from war to property, from vanity to science, from conquest to luxury."[31] Substitutionalist equality, the idea that we can effectively stand in for one another, becomes the conceptual norm: "This is a strange world; it is one in which individuals are grown up before they have been born; in which boys are men before they have been children; a world where neither mother, nor sister, nor wife exist."[32] Benhabib argues that it is not simply misogynist prejudice that explains women's exclusion—the very constitution of a sphere of discourse "bans the female from history to the realm of nature, from the light of the public to the interior

---

29. Hobbes quoted in Benhabib, "Generalized and the Concrete Other," 156.

30. Benhabib, "Generalized and the Concrete Other," 156.

31. To be clear, this myth-making activity was highly successful in the realm of political philosophy—from Locke to Rawls and Kohlberg. Different kinds of myth-making activities adorned the practices of conquest, war, and vanity—which may have been transformed in theory but not in the horrific practices of empire building.

32. Benhabib, "Generalized and the Concrete Other," 157.

of the household, from the civilizing effect of culture to the repetitious burden of nurture and reproduction."[33]

Many modernist thinkers who valorize the moral domain of justice view the domestic sphere as dangerous. It is not coincidental that this sphere is also associated with women. Imagining the private sphere as timeless drudgery creates a peculiar kind of sacred space. As Maurice Bloch shows, formalization creates the ambience of the eternal by means of limitation and repetition. When symbols are removed from a highly interactive discursive field, they take on a new meaning-less form.[34] Situating the domestic sphere as a realm of ritualized and repetitious space, the space takes on a timeless and almost irrelevant quality. It is not surprising that the private sphere was imagined as including the supposed doldrums of domestic life as well as the effervescence of religion.

Taking her lead from Gilligan's critique of Kohlberg, Benhabib examines the apparent incompatibility of two moral perspectives: the Kohlbergian standpoint of the "generalized" and the contextualized "concrete" other, inspired by the work of Gilligan and her collaborators. The generalized other focuses on what we have in common and is governed by the norms of formal equality and reciprocity.[35] The standpoint of the concrete other requires that we see that individuals have a concrete history, identity, and affective-emotional constitution. Our relation to the other is governed by the norms of equity and complementary reciprocity. In this model, our differences complement rather than exclude. The moral categories of the generalized other include respect, duty, and dignity (our humanity) while the categories of the concrete other include responsibility, bonding, and sharing with the corresponding feelings of love, care and sympathy, and solidarity (our history and context).[36]

---

33. Benhabib, "Generalized and the Concrete Other," 157.

34. For the impact of this transformation, see Alasdair MacIntyre, *After Virtue: A Study in Moral Theory* (Notre Dame, IN: University of Notre Dame Press, 1981).

35. "Each is entitled to expect and to assume from us what we can expect and assume from him or her." Benhabib, "Generalized and Concrete Other," 159.

36. Benhabib, "Generalized and the Concrete Other," 159.

While Benhabib is not claiming to resolve the difference between these two standpoints, she argues that "ignoring the standpoint of the concrete other leads to epistemic incoherence in universalistic moral theories."[37] When we make sharp distinctions between public and private interests we end up with an identity devoid of history and context. If we are asked to surrender our connection to the private realm, the very place that core aspects of our collective identities are nurtured and sustained, our public sense of self is vastly diminished. Benhabib argues that reciprocity is simply not possible with a self that is constituted without particularity, without history or context. There's no other to be reciprocal with. Following Habermas, Benhabib calls the standpoint of the generalized other a "monological" model of moral reasoning:

> A definition of the self that is restricted to the standpoint of the generalized other becomes incoherent and cannot individuate among selves. Without assuming the standpoint of the concrete other, no coherent universalizability test can be carried out, for we lack the necessary epistemic information to judge my moral situation to be "like" or "unlike" yours.[38]

Taking her lead from Habermas, Benhabib argues that a universalistic moral theory requires a reversibility of perspectives that takes differences seriously. Conceptual devices designed to curtail the intermingling of public and private interests may deactivate certain kinds of differences but may "leave all our prejudices, misunderstandings and hostilities" intact.[39] Without the actual voice of the other, without their unrestricted participation, moral deliberation is threatened by its own incoherent self-limitations. A deliberative conception of morality institutes an actual dialogue among selves who are both equal moral agents and concrete others with tangible differences. In closing, Benhabib makes four critical points: first, the moral standpoint must be construed not as a hypothetical thought process but as an actual dialogue; second, no epistemic restrictions should be placed

37. Benhabib, "Generalized and the Concrete Other," 161.
38. Benhabib, "Generalized and the Concrete Other," 164–165.
39. Benhabib, "Generalized and the Concrete Other," 167.

upon moral reasoning and moral disputation; third, there can be no privileged subjected matter; and, fourth, moral agents can introduce metaconsiderations about the very conditions and constraints under which dialogue takes place.[40] The model espoused by Benhabib is reflexively critical of restrictive formalizations—whether in the form of magical thinking, myth, or ritual. Her model welcomes moral feelings but is cautious to emphasize that moral conversations are reasoning processes that prize working through strong emotions rather than leaving them intact. In this sense, morality and moral deliberation openly challenge the ideological aspects of human interaction that are redescribed in our key categories.[41] Benhabib's brief overview of the exclusions of the moral domain further explains why revisioning evil is necessary. If the traditional concept of evil is rooted in blind spots and exclusions, recasting evil as dangers and aversions aims to rethink the concept without the same set of exclusions.

Example 2: The Affair of the Scarf

One of the more contentious aspects of modernization is the separation between religion and politics, a separation that coincides with the separation of public and private and the ensuing arthritic conception of morality that followed. The fragile wall between religion and politics, if it was ever much of a wall to begin with, is proving to be much more porous than the secular imagination thought. Increasingly, political theorists are renegotiating the meaning of religion in the public square. As Benhabib notes, "Women's bodies in particular have become the site of symbolic confrontations between a re-essentialized understanding of religious and cultural difference and the forces of state power, whether in their civic-republican,

---

40. Benhabib, "Generalized and the Concrete Other," 169.

41. Just to be clear, morality as ideology critique opposes the processes and forms of interaction that are redescribed by the key categories. Morality opposes coercion in human relationships not "magical thinking" or "mythmaking" as analytic concepts.

liberal-democratic or multicultural form."[42] This re-essentialization of religion emerges in the context of the ongoing destabilization of identities and traditions that comes with capitalist exchange and the restructuring of collective life into spheres like science, politics, and religion. Through these upheavals, identities and traditions are reinvented as a matter of course. Benhabib is critical of these homogenizing or essentializing tendencies in politics, what she comes to call "political theology." Benhabib uses this term because it captures the refusal to accept deliberation as a means of adjudicating competing interests.

In the context of Benhabib's work, political theology refers to the deterritorialization of religion, the re-imagining of religion without a geographic territory and national sovereignty. Reterritorialized religion not only challenges the authority of the traditional nation-state but also dislodges the national sense of collective identity:[43] "Paradoxically, by undermining the authority of the nation-state the deterritorialization of religion under conditions of globalization evokes memories of pre-modernity, and enflames the power of the tribes which are now busy renewing themselves with the means provided by decentralized means of postmodern communication, exchange, commerce and information."[44] As Benhabib shows, the so-called "scarf affair" has become the site of a transnational struggle implicating the sovereignty of the secular nation-state, constitutional negotiations, and the symbolic markings of the female body. Her essay compares three judicial responses to the scarf—in France, Germany, and Turkey. In each instance, the judicial responses reference national idealizations described in terms very close to purity and danger. Drawing on insights from moral theory, Benhabib provides a critique of the exclusions created or preserved by these court decisions.

In France in 1989, three scarf-wearing Muslim girls were expelled from their school in Creil (Oise). Twenty-three Muslim girls were expelled from their schools in November 1996, and in March 2004 the French National Assembly passed a law banning the wearing of the

---

42. Benhabib, "Return of Political Theology," 453.
43. Benhabib, "Return of Political Theology," 456.
44. Benhabib, "Return of Political Theology," 456.

scarf ("*la voile*") and the bearing of "all ostentatious signs of religious belonging in the public sphere." The Commission headed by Bernard Stasi made the claim that the wearing of the scarf constituted a growing political threat of Islam to the values of *laïcité*.[45] As Benhabib puts it, the French Republic's balance between respecting the individual's right to freedom of conscience and religion and religious neutrality was so fragile that it "took only the actions of a handful of teenagers to expose this fragility."[46] The girls' voices were not heard much in this debate. Benhabib identifies the issues as follows:

> Even if the girls involved were not adults and in the eyes of the law were still under the tutelage of their families, it is reasonable to assume that at the ages of 15 and 16, they could account for themselves and their actions. Had their voices been heard and listened to, it would have become clear that the meaning of the wearing of the scarf itself was changing from being a religious act to one of cultural defiance and increasing politicization. Ironically, it was the very egalitarian norms of the French public educational system which brought these girls out of the patriarchal structures of the home and into the French public sphere and gave them the confidence and the ability to *resignify the wearing of the scarf*.[47]

The claim that "the scarf" is essentially a religious symbol and that a particular religion is essentially a political threat (a potential contagion that might undermine the very fabric of the state) is an exercise in magical thinking. The political maneuvers here are those of formalization, a ban on particular articles of clothing without options for deliberation. Benhabib formulates the moral problem: "To assume that the meaning of their actions is purely one of religious defiance of the secular state denigrates these women's own capacity to define the meaning of their own actions and, ironically, reimprisons them within the walls of patriarchal meaning from which they are trying to escape."[48]

---

45. Benhabib, "Return of Political Theology," 457.
46. Benhabib, "Return of Political Theology," 458.
47. Benhabib, "Return of Political Theology," 459.
48. Benhabib, "Return of Political Theology," 459.

In September 2003, a similar decision was reached in Germany. The German Supreme Court acknowledged Fereshta Ludin's fundamental right to wear a headscarf and express her belonging to the Muslim faith community but failed to shield these rights by transferring final say on the matter to democratic legislatures. Baden-Würtemberg's Minister of Education, Annete Schavan, argued that "The headscarf ... also stands for cultural segregation, and thus is a political symbol [which puts at risk] social peace."[49] Since Germany is not a laic state but one wedded to the Christian-Western tradition (*Christlich-Abendländische*) in which Protestant, Catholic and Jewish institutions are financed directly by taxes, legislation singled out Islamic symbols as "inherently political and provocative."[50] Such blatantly anti-Islamic legislation essentializes meaning presumed to be intrinsic to certain symbols, giving them an aura of timelessness and reducing any possible response to such symbols as anything other than reactionary.

The last case Benhabib discusses is that of the Turkish "turban affair." In February 2008, the ruling Turkish party (Adalet ve Kalkinma Partisi) decided to reform the law that banned the wearing of headscarves and turbans in institutions of higher learning. In June 2008, the Turkish Constitutional Court overturned the new legislation, arguing that it was subversive of the secular nature of the Turkish state. One piece of the proposed legislation pertained to teaching and education and read "No language other than Turkish can be taught ... in any institutions of learning and instruction as a mother tongue." Benhabib describes the implications:

> This is a militant assertion of the "homogeneity" of the *ethnos* upon which the *demos*, the political nation, is based. It reveals the tension between the *demos* of the Turkish republic which consists of Turkish citizens, regardless of their religion, ethnic creed and color on the one hand and the imaginary unity and supposed homogeneity of the *ethnos*, a national which is supposed to have no other mother language than Turkish, on the other.[51]

---

49. Benhabib, "Return of Political Theology," 461.
50. Benhabib, "Return of Political Theology," 461.
51. Benhabib, "Return of Political Theology," 463.

The "imaginary unity" here is the work of extensive myth-making, a tactic for creating unity out of the frays and tatters of contradictory and contested identities. The purity of this essentialized *ethnos* is described as threatened by uncontained others.

As Benhabib argues, the headscarf debate centers time and time again around the pluralization of identities in a post-nationalist and democratic society. A robust pluralism defends the right to wear a headscarf and also the right not to wear a headscarf. Viewing the headscarf as a political symbol requiring state regulation demeans and ignores the rather ordinary continual renegotiations of symbolic meanings. "For the girls and women involved, the headscarf and turban are no longer simply expressions of Muslim humility but symbols of an embattled identity and signs of public defiance."[52]

These political moves aiming to restrict deliberation and garner support for a more reactive and unthinking response run contrary to a conception of morality that defends the importance of ongoing conversation and deliberation. Benhabib borrows Jacques Derrida's phrase "democratic iterations" to express the very changing flow of meaning, effectively noting that every claim to tradition is a reinvention of that tradition and that every attempt to preserve homogeneity is a fabrication of collective identity.

Conclusion

From the viewpoint of morality, dangers and aversions are defined in terms of processes that foreclose full participation in a complicated human community. In this sense, morality both signifies a sense of violation and intuitively anticipates a process for the open-ended negotiation of norms. Whereas magical thinking puts things in their place by means of essentialization, moral thinking opens the world of symbols to processes of resignification. Meaning, then, is a process of mutual esteem and recognition. Classification systems rooted in cosmologies sustained by a hierarchy of elites resist modification and often punish deviance. A deliberative model of morality readily

---

52. Benhabib, "Return of Political Theology," 465.

accepts if not encourages the re-signifying of our symbol systems according to our shared interests and desires. Just as formalization restricts options, morality obligates people to consider respectfully and reciprocally the viewpoints of others. Mythmaking creates frameworks that rank and prioritize value and meaning by means of concealing the powers of authorization from view. Moral discourse, on the other hand, attempts to criticize powers and authorities that exclude, denigrate, or marginalize others.

That being said, magical thinking, mythmaking, ritualization, and strong emotions each in their own way challenge existing authorities and powers. They express negotiations and renegotiations with culture. As dynamic forces, we cannot rule out their power to humanize or express moral intuitions. I'm not drawing an oppositional line between morality and myth. Morality challenges the spellbinding power of myth and the concealed interests of mythmaking, but this does not mean that myth and mythmaking do not contain moral intuitions or sentiments.

For example, the powers of magical thinking, classification, ritual and ritualization, myth and mythmaking, and strong emotions are displayed with polished clarity in many of the debates and conflicts concerning Indigenous sovereignty and Canada, located on the land that is also called Turtle Island. When Leroy Little Bear concludes that "Canada is a pretend nation," he is articulating a moral critique and making explicit how settler colonial classification, myth, and ritual have replaced interactive relationships with administrative documents, disconnected from people and places.[53]

A consideration of moral discourse is key for our purposes here because of its emphasis on dangers and aversions. Morality is rooted in our collective interactions, as they are entwined with our identities and our experience of dignity. Additionally, it encompasses our sense of obligation and responsibility as well as the need for respect and reciprocity in the process of adjudicating moral and legal norms. Morality also takes a critical form when coercive or ideological forces violate the protective shell of moral relationships. The core focus

---

53. Leroy Little Bear, "Canada is a Pretend Nation," in Ladner and Tait, *Surviving Canada*, 36–42.

of moral criticism is harm. Moral norms are protective measures designed to minimize harm and risk. The emphasis on evil as dangers and aversions allows us to see morality not simply as arbitrary judgement about good and evil but as a process of collective reflection and criticism. Morality registers dangers, charts aversions, and as a collective system of interaction, aims to rectify failures, exclusions, and harms.

Chapter 7

Conclusion

It is time for our experiment to come to an end. We have defined evil as perceived dangers and aversions, and, by thinking about dangers and aversions with a variety of key categories, we have explored the multiple ways in which human beings classify the world. As we end our course of study, we should consider what we have learned, what questions remain, and where we go next.

One of the animating thoughts underlying this primer concerns a distinction between two very different imaginings of evil. On the one hand, we have a conception of evil that defines it in very modern terms. A modern conception of evil is imagined as the violation of human rights, defined succinctly as atrocity. On the other hand, we have evil imagined more along the lines of dirt—what Mary Douglas theorizes as matter out of place. In this latter formulation, evil is associated with impurity, and that impurity is narrativized and entwined within a larger cosmology.

In an earlier version of my course on evil, my students and I experimented with a developmental thesis that religious notions of evil preceded modern notions of evil. This provocation suggested that children start with an intuitive sense of clean and dirty, which grows into a more mature distinction between right and wrong. The following year, we reversed the thesis to suggest that religious notions of evil are derivatives of intuitive moral notions of evil. In posing these kinds of questions at the beginning of the course, I wasn't so much looking for answers as encouraging students to think about how they are thinking about evil. Over time I have become less inclined to see this "which came first, the chicken or the egg?" approach as helpful. These two imaginings of evil are not genealogically related but instead belong to different registers or different worlds of discourse.

As mentioned earlier, one of the most curious aspects of the novel *Dracula* is the way in which the protagonists sidestep their moral impulses in order to eliminate what they come to regard as an abomination. Combined with his knowledge of medicine, Van Helsing's narratives about vampires establish him as a primary mythmaker in the novel. Dracula comes to be approached in a highly ritualized fashion, such that his presence invokes disgust and his touch invokes shame. The key categories are at work on almost every page of the book. We see in this gothic novel a desire to cleanse and purify in a way that overrides the characters' moral impulses not to mutilate or kill. In a sense, the novel gives us a vivid sense of how pollution regulations replace morality. While as a reader I am carried along by the enjoyable ebb and flow of this story, as a cultural critic, I'm terrified by it. I'm less terrified by Dracula than I am by the heroes. The heroic task of purification replaces the subjective humanity of others with an objective consciousness of dirt. Dracula is treated with nothing short of furious contempt. He becomes matter out of place. As such, he must be obliterated.

The pattern of interaction depicted in *Dracula* is extreme when aligned next to most of the other illustrations in this course of study, but it is not unfamiliar. The corpse handlers in the Cantonese village become filthy pariahs. Women in the rural Turkish village are perpetually caught in a web of shame, while domestic life in Buddhist hagiographic literature is re-cast as cramped, disgusting, and unfree. The simulated dialogue of Christian witnessing strategically aims to tear asunder a sense of well-being and to replace it with a sense of dread and brokenness. I used each of these examples to illustrate one of the key categories, but without much additional work, we can see most of the key categories at work in each and every case.

In the end, these concepts have helped us in our task of redescribing evil as dangers and aversions with a new vocabulary. They also point to how dangers and become "real," how the transcendental social gains a degree of veridicality or realism. We haven't explained dangers and aversions in particular, but we get a sense of the techniques and social forces that are at work in the fabrication of the shared norms and fantasies that constitute our social lives. We have a better sense of how we create borders of inside and out, how we create collective identities, how we concoct the extraordinary out of the ordinary, and how we regulate relations between one another. I designed this primer as something of a field guide. With the help of a few key categories, the book assists readers in identifying dangers and aversions in the wild, on the street, and in the classroom. The reason for creating a catalogue of dangers and aversions is that doing so helps us better perceive and describe how we interact with one another and gives us a better sense of the scope and range of human relations. The key categories alongside illustrations work like puzzle pieces interlock to provide a broader view.

Over the years, my students have suggested a number of topics and key categories that could be added to the course: the demonic, the righteous mind, violence and harm, the fear of death, power, deviance, extremism, race and racism, cults and the occult. Other students have been less persuaded by the approach emphasizing dangers and aversions and, instead, urged a turn towards "actual evil" and "real religion." Every so often, a group of students also request a larger section on *Harry Potter*.[1]

Where do we go next? We can discern two notions of evil: a moral conception of dangers and aversions and a religious conception of dangers and aversions. I think the next step, then, is not an examination of how we form collectives or make symbols appear holy (or not-evil), but a consideration of how we imagine our relationships in the first place—how we transform people into things and things into people. A religious notion of evil trades in illustrations of dangerous essences and captures how we create, maintain, and renegotiate relationships along essentializing lines. A moral notion of evil focuses on our experience of dignity as well as our collectively generated obligations and responsibilities. In a future study, what we have been referring to as moral and religious conceptions of evil here could be recalibrated to study what we might propose to call subjective, intersubjective, and objective conceptions of evil.

---

1. Scholars of evil often have similar impulses—wanting to talk about the "real thing" as well as travel down a distracting rabbit hole for fun. Adam Morton's *On Evil* readily identifies the reality of evil and has a section on *Buffy the Vampire Slayer*. Adam Morton, *On Evil* (New York: Routledge, 2004).

Now that we have a better understanding of how we create, maintain, and dissolve shared social worlds, maybe we can put these insights to more precise use by studying how relationships between people are transformed into relationships between things—a study in objectification or perhaps reification. An objective conception of evil could be a conception of evil that defines evil not simply in terms of dangers and aversions (dirt, pollution, impurity) but in terms of the intersubjective processes that distort or deny agency or personhood. In other words, we might study the social processes that undermine the subjectivities at work in creating shared social worlds. Equally important would be how we transform objects into entities or how we interact with our dreams or our shared fantasies.

The key categories I have introduced should be helpful in understanding the process of transforming a subject into an object and the process of transforming an object into a subject. We see throughout many of the illustrations that people are transformed into things: the corpse handler is transformed into a pariah, the Christian into a creature of unfortunate heredity, or the non-practicing Muslim into an unbeliever. The painful and ongoing everyday reality of misogyny, racism, and colonialism demonstrate the power of the elements we've discussed—classification and magical thinking, ritual, myth, and strong emotions—to transform people into things. Meanwhile, morality runs contrary to this tendency. In moral discourses, ideological critique aims to create time and space for those whose voices have been denied. In this way, they are subjectivizing discourses that attempt to restore humanity to those who have been dehumanized. All of these elements, each in their own way and taken together, can make us more aware of our fragility and our shared subjectivities. It is that awareness that helps us provide our own answers to the question I ask in my course: "What do (and don't) you think about when you think about evil?"

Further Reading

General Works

Bloch, Maurice. "Why Religion is Nothing Special but is Central." *In and Out of Each Other's Bodies: Theory of Mind, Evolution, Truth, and the Nature of the Social*, 23–40. Boulder, CO: Paradigm Publishers, 2013.

Braun, Willi and Russell T. McCutcheon, eds. *Guide to the Study of Religion*. New York: Continuum, 2000.

Douglas, Mary. *Purity and Danger: An Analysis of Concepts of Pollution and Taboo*. New York: Routledge, 2002.

Juschka, Darlene M. *Political Bodies/Body Politic: The Semiotics of Gender*. London: Equinox, 2009.

Lincoln, Bruce. *Discourse and the Construction of Society*, 2nd edition. Chicago, IL: University of Chicago Press, 2014.

MacKendrick, Kenneth G. "Evil in World Religions at the University of Manitoba (2002–2008): An Introduction and Provocation." *Golem: Journal of Religion and Monsters* 3, no. 1 (2009), 37–55. Retrieved from www.criticaltheoryofreligion.org/wp-content/uploads/2018/08/GOLEM3-1-2009_MacKendrick.pdf.

McCutcheon, Russell T. *Studying Religion: An Introduction*, 2nd edition. New York: Routledge, 2019.

Smith, Jonathan Z. *Imagining Religion: From Babylon to Jonestown*. Chicago, IL: University of Chicago Press, 1982.

Classification

Douglas, Mary. "Introduction" and "Secular Defilement." *Purity and Danger: An Analysis of Concepts of Pollution and Taboo*, 1–7, 36–50. New York: Routledge, 2002.

Smith, Jonathan Z. "Classification." In *Guide to the Study of Religion*, 35-44. Edited by Willi Braun and Russell T. McCutcheon. New York: Continuum, 2000.

Magical Thinking

Nemeroff, Carol and Paul Rozin. "The Makings of the Magical Mind: The Nature and Function of Sympathetic Magical Thinking." In *Imagining the Impossible: Magical, Scientific, and Religious Thinking in Children*, 1-34. Edited by Karl S. Rosengren, Carl N. Johnson, and Paul L. Harris. Cambridge: Cambridge University Press, 2000.

Rosengren, Karl S. and Jason A. French. "Magical Thinking." In *The Oxford Handbook of the Development of Imagination*, 42-27. Edited by Marjorie Taylor. New York: Oxford University Press, 2013.

Subbotsky, Eugene. *Magic and the Mind: Mechanisms, Functions, and Development of Magical Thinking and Behavior*. Oxford: Oxford University Press, 2010.

Rituals and Ritualization

Bloch, Maurice. "Symbols, Song, Dance and Features of Articulation or Is Religion an Extreme Form of Traditional Authority?" *European Journal of Sociology/Archives Européennes de Sociologie* 15, no. 1 (1974), 55-81.

Bloch, Maurice. "The Past and the Present in the Past." *Man* 12, no. 2 (1977), 278-292.

Bloch, Maurice. "Rituals and Deference." In *Essays on Cultural Transmission*, 123-121. Oxford: BERG, 2005.

Myth and Mythmaking

Barthes, Roland. *Mythologies*. Translated by Annette Lavers. New York: Hill and Wang, 1972.

Lincoln, Bruce. *Theorizing Myth: Narrative, Ideology, and Scholarship*. Chicago, IL: University of Chicago Press, 1999.

McCutcheon, Russell T. "Myth." In *Guide to the Study of Religion*, 190-208. Edited by Willi Braun and Russell T. McCutcheon. New York: Continuum, 2000.

Strong Emotions (shame and disgust)

Miller, William Ian. *The Anatomy of Disgust.* Cambridge, MA: Harvard University Press, 1998.

Nussbaum, Martha C. *Hiding from Humanity: Disgust, Shame, and the Law.* Princeton, NJ: Princeton University Press, 2006.

Rochat, Philippe. "Shame and Self-Knowledge." *Others in Mind: Social Origins of Self-Consciousness*, 105–117. Cambridge: Cambridge University Press 2009.

Rozin, P., J. Haidt, and C. R. McCauley. "Disgust." In *Handbook of Emotions*, 3rd edition, 757–776. Edited by M. Lewis, J. M. Haviland-Jones, and L. Feldman Barrett. New York: Guilford Press, 2008.

Morality

Benhabib, Seyla. *The Claims of Culture: Equality and Diversity in the Global Era.* Princeton, NJ: Princeton University Press, 2002.

Benhabib, Seyla. *Dignity in Adversity: Human Rights in Troubled Times.* Cambridge: Polity, 2011.

Habermas, Jürgen, "The Concept of Human Dignity and the Realistic Utopia of Human Rights." *The Crisis of the European Union*, 71–100. Translated by Ciaran Cronin. Malden, MA: Polity Press, 2012.

Habermas, Jürgen. *Moral Consciousness and Communicative Action.* Translated by Christian Lenhardt and Shierry Weber Nicholsen. Cambridge, MA: MIT Press, 1990.

References

Adorno, Theodor W. *The Jargon of Authenticity*. Translated by Knut Tarnowski and Frederic Will. Evanston, IL: Northwestern University Press, 1973.

Arendt, Hannah. *Eichmann in Jerusalem: A Report on the Banality of Evil*. New York: Penguin Classics, 1993.

Armstrong, Karen. *A Short History of Myth*. Toronto: Vintage Canada, 2006.

Arnal, William E. and Russell T. McCutcheon. *The Sacred Is the Profane: The Political Nature of "Religion."* New York: Oxford University Press, 2013.

Asad, Talal. *Genealogies of Religion: Discipline and Reasons of Power in Christianity and Islam*. Baltimore, MD: Johns Hopkins University Press, 1997.

Asad, Talal. *Secular Translations: Nation-State, Modern Self, and Calculative Reason*. New York: Columbia University Press, 2018.

Baker, Kelly J. *The Zombies are Coming: The Realities of the Zombie Apocalypse in American Culture*, revised and expanded edition. Chapel Hill, NC: Blue Crow Books, 2020.

Baldanzi, Jessica and Hussein Rashid, eds., *Ms. Marvel's America: No Normal*. Jackson, MS: University Press of Mississippi, 2020.

Bale, Rachael. "The Disturbing Secret Behind the World's Most Expensive Coffee." *National Geographic*. April 29, 2016. Retrieved from www.nationalgeographic.com/animals/article/160429-kopi-luwak-captive-civet-coffee-Indonesia.

Beal, Timothy K. *Religion and Its Monsters*. New York: Routledge, 2002.

Benhabib, Seyla. *The Claims of Culture: Equality and Diversity in the Global Era*. Princeton, NJ: Princeton University Press, 2002.

Benhabib, Seyla. *Critique, Norm, and Utopia: A Study of the Foundations of Critical Theory*. New York: Columbia University Press, 1986.

Benhabib, Seyla. "The Return of Political Theology: The Scarf Affair in Comparative Constitutional Perspective in France, Germany, and Turkey." *Philosophy and Social Criticism* 36, no. 3–4 (2010), 451–471.

Benhabib, Seyla. *Situating the Self: Gender, Community and Postmodernism in Contemporary Ethics*. New York: Routledge, 1992.

Benhabib, Seyla and Fred R. Dallmayr, eds. *The Communicative Ethics Controversy*. Cambridge, MA: MIT Press, 1990.

Bernstein, Richard J. *The Abuse of Evil: The Corruption of Politics and Religion since 9/11.* Malden, MA: Polity, 2005.

Bernstein, Richard J. *Radical Evil: A Philosophical Interrogation.* Malden, MA: Blackwell Publishers, 2002.

Bloch, Maurice. "Symbols, Song, Dance and Features of Articulation or Is Religion an Extreme Form of Traditional Authority?" *European Journal of Sociology/Archives Européennes de Sociologie* 15, no. 1 (1974), 55–81.

Bloch, Maurice. *In and Out of Each Other's Bodies: Theory of Mind, Evolution, Truth, and the Nature of the Social.* Boulder, CO: Paradigm Publishers, 2013.

Bloch, Maurice. *Essays on Cultural Transmission.* Oxford: Berg, 2005.

Bloudoof-Indelicato, Mollie. "Beaver Butts Emit Goo used for Vanilla Flavoring." National Geographic. October 1, 2013. Retrieved from www.nationalgeographic.com/animals/article/beaver-butt-goo-vanilla-flavoring.

Bomgardner, Melody M. "The Problem with Vanilla." *Chemical and Engineering News* 94, no. 36 (2016). Retrieved from https://cen.acs.org/articles/94/i36/problem-vanilla.html.

Bowker, John. *Problems of Suffering in Religions of the World.* Cambridge: Cambridge University Press, 1970.

Bowler, Kate. *Blessed: A History of the American Prosperity Gospel.* Oxford: Oxford University Press, 2013.

Braude, Ann. *Radical Spirits: Spiritualism and Women's Rights in Nineteenth-Century America,* 2nd edition. Bloomington, IN: Indiana University Press, 2001.

Braun, Willi and Russell T. McCutcheon, eds. *Guide to the Study of Religion.* New York: Continuum, 2000.

Cenkner, William, ed. *Evil and the Response of World Religion.* St. Paul's, MN: Paragon House, 1997.

Chidester, David. *Empire of Religion Imperialism and Comparative Religion.* Chicago, IL: University of Chicago Press, 2014.

Chidester, David. *Savage Systems: Colonialism and Comparative Religion in Southern Africa.* Charlottesville: University Press of Virginia Press, 1996.

Cote-Meek, Sheila. *Colonized Classrooms: Racism, Trauma and Resistance in Post-Secondary Education.* Winnipeg: Fernwood Publishing, 2014.

Dawkins, Richard. *The God Delusion.* Boston, MA: Houghton Mifflin Harcourt, 2008.

Dawkins, Richard. *The Greatest Show on Earth: The Evidence for Evolution.* New York: Free Press, 2009.

Delaney, Carol. "Seeds of Honor, Fields of Shame." In *Honor and Shame and the Unity of the Mediterranean,* 35–48. Edited by David Gilmore. Washington, DC: American Anthropological Association, 1987.

Delaney, Carol. *The Seed and Soil: Gender and Cosmology in Turkish Village Society.* Berkeley, CA: University of California Press, 1991.

Dews, Peter. *The Idea of Evil.* Malden, MA: Wiley-Blackwell, 2013.

DiAngelo, Robin. *White Fragility: Why It's So Hard for White People to Talk about Racism.* Boston, MA: Beacon Press, 2018.

Douglas, Mary. *Purity and Danger: An Analysis of Concepts of Pollution and Taboo.* New York: Routledge, 2002.

Eilberg-Schwartz, and Wendy Doniger. *Off With Her Head! The Denial of Women's Identity in Myth, Religion, and Culture.* Berkeley, CA: University of California Press, 1995.

Frankfurter, David. *Evil Incarnate: Rumors of Demonic Conspiracy and Satanic Abuse in History.* Princeton, NJ: Princeton University Press, 2006.

Garrett, Greg. *Holy Superheroes!,* revised and expanded edition. Louisville, KY: Westminster John Knox Press, 2008.

Habermas, Jürgen. *The Crisis of the European Union.* Translated by Ciaran Cronin. Malden, MA: Polity Press, 2012.

Habermas, Jürgen. *Communication and the Evolution of Society.* Translated by Thomas McCarthy. Boston, MA: Beacon Press, 1979.

Habermas, Jürgen. *Moral Consciousness and Communicative Action.* Translated by Christian Lenhardt and Shierry Weber Nicholsen. Cambridge, MA: MIT Press, 1990.

Habermas, Jürgen. *Postmetaphysical Thinking: Philosophical Essays.* Translated by William Mark Hohengarten. Cambridge, MA: MIT Press, 1992.

Habermas, Jürgen. *The Theory of Communicative Action, 2 vols.* Translated by Thomas McCarthy. Boston, MA: Beacon Press, 1984/1987.

Harding, Susan Friend. *The Book of Jerry Falwell: Fundamentalist Language and Politics.* Princeton, NJ: Princeton University Press, 2000.

Harlan, Lindsey. "Perfection and Devotion: Sati Tradition in Rajasthan." In *Sati, the Blessing and the Curse: The Burning of Wives in India,* 79–91. Edited by John Stratton Hawley. New York: Oxford University Press, 1994.

Harlan, Lindsey. *Religion and Rajput Women: The Ethic of Protection in Contemporary Narratives.* Berkeley, CA: University of California Press, 1992.

Harris, Paul. *Children and Imagination.* Malden, MA: Blackwell Publishers, 2000.

Harris, Paul. *Trusting What You're Told: How Children Learn from Others.* Cambridge, MA: Belknap Press, 2015.

Havkin-Frenkel, Daphna, Faith C. Belanger, Debra Y. J. Booth, Kathryn E. Galasso, Francis P. Tangel, and Carlos Javier Hernández Gayosso. "A Comprehensive Study of Composition and Evaluation of Vanilla Extracts in US Retails Stores." *Handbook of Vanilla Science and*

Technology, 220–234. Edited by Daphna Havkin-Frenkel and Faith C. Belanger. Malden, MA: Blackwell Publishing, 2011.

Henkel, Heiko. "'Between Belief and Unbelief Lies the Performance of Salāt': Meaning and Efficacy of a Muslim Ritual." *Journal of the Royal Anthropological Institute* 11 (2005), 487–507.

Hewitt, Marsha A. *Critical Theory of Religion: A Feminist Analysis*. Minneapolis, MN: Fortress Press, 1999.

Hopwood, Nick, Rebecca Flemming, and Lauren Kassell, eds. *Reproduction: Antiquity to the Present Day*. Cambridge: Cambridge University Press, 2018.

Hughes, Aaron W. *Comparison: A Critical Primer*. Sheffield: Equinox, 2017.

Humphrey, Caroline and James Laidlaw. *The Archetypal Actions of Ritual: A Theory of Ritual Illustrated by the Jain Rite of Worship*. Oxford: Oxford University Press, 1994.

Jentz, Paul. *Seven Myths of Native American History*. Indianapolis, IN: Hackett Publishing Company, 2018.

Juschka, Darlene M. *Political Bodies/Body Politic: The Semiotics of Gender*. London: Equinox, 2009.

Kimmerer, Robin Wall. *Gathering Moss: A Natural and Cultural History of Mosses*. Corvallis, OR: Oregon State University Press, 2003.

Kippenberg, Hans G. *Discovering Religious History in the Modern Age*. Translated by Barbara Harshaw. Princeton, NJ: Princeton University Press, 2002.

Koslofsky, Craig. "Offshoring the Invisible World? American Ghosts, Witches, and Demons in the Early Enlightenment." *Critical Research on Religion* 9, no. 2 (2021), 126–141.

Ladner, Kiera L. and Myra Tait, eds. *Surviving Canada: Indigenous Peoples Celebrate 150 Years of Betrayal*. Winnipeg: ARP Books, 2017.

Lakoff, George and Mark Johnson. *Metaphors We Live By*. Chicago, IL: University of Chicago Press, 2003.

Lara, Mía Pía, ed. *Rethinking Evil: Contemporary Perspectives*. Berkeley, CA: University of California Press, 2001.

Lara, Mía Pía. *Narrating Evil: A Postmetaphysical Theory of Reflective Judgment*. New York: Columbia University Press, 2007.

Lawson, Thomas E. and Robert N. McCauley. *Rethinking Religion: Connecting Cognition and Culture*. Cambridge: Cambridge University Press, 1993.

Laycock, Joseph P. *Dangerous Games: What the Moral Panic over Role-Playing Games Says about Play, Religion, and Imagined Worlds*. Oakland, CA: University of California Press, 2015.

Lepselter, Susan. *The Resonance of Unseen Things: Poetics, Power, Captivity, and UFOs in the American Uncanny*. Ann Arbor, MI: University of Michigan Press, 2016.

Lincoln, Bruce. *Apples and Oranges: Explorations In, On, and With Comparison.* Chicago, IL: University of Chicago Press, 2018.

Lincoln, Bruce. *Authority: Construction and Corrosion.* Chicago, IL: University of Chicago Press, 1994.

Lincoln, Bruce. *Discourse and the Construction of Society,* 2nd edition. Chicago, IL: University of Chicago Press, 2014.

Lincoln, Bruce. *Theorizing Myth: Narrative, Ideology, and Scholarship.* Chicago, IL: University of Chicago Press, 1999.

Loewen, Nathan R. B. *Beyond the Problem of Evil: Derrida and Anglophone Philosophy of Religion.* Lanham, MD: Lexington Books, 2018.

Luhrmann, Tanya. *When God Talks Back: Understanding the American Evangelical Relationship with God.* New York: Alfred A. Knopf, 2012.

Lyden, John and Ken Derry. *The Myth Awakens: Canon, Conservatism, and Fan Reception of Star Wars.* Eugene, OR: Cascade Books, 2018.

MacIntyre, Alasdair. *After Virtue: A Study in Moral Theory.* Notre Dame, IN: University of Notre Dame Press, 1981.

Mandel, Naomi. "Rethinking 'After Auschwitz': Against a Rhetoric of the Unspeakable in Holocaust Writing." *Boundary 2* 28, no. 2 (2001), 203–228.

Matuštík, Martin Beck. *Radical Evil and the Scarcity of Hope: Postsecular Meditations.* Bloomington, IN: Indiana University Press, 2008.

Masuzawa, Tomoko. *The Invention of World Religions; Or, How European Universalism Was Preserved in the Language of Pluralism.* Chicago, IL: University of Chicago Press, 2005.

McCallum, Mary Jane Logan and Adele Perry. *Structures of Indifference: An Indigenous Life and Death in a Canadian City.* Winnipeg: University of Manitoba Press, 2018.

McCutcheon, Russell T. *Critics Not Caretakers: Redescribing the Public Study of Religion.* Albany, NY: SUNY Press, 2001.

McCutcheon, Russell T. *The Discipline of Religion: Structure, Meaning, Rhetoric.* New York: Routledge, 2003.

McCutcheon, Russell T. *Manufacturing Religion: The Discourse on Sui Generis Religion and the Politics of Nostalgia.* Oxford: Oxford University Press, 2003.

McCutcheon, Russell T. *Studying Religion: An Introduction,* 2nd edition. New York: Routledge, 2019.

Milne, Pamela J. "What Shall We Do With Judith? A Feminist Reassessment of a Biblical Heroine." *Semeia* 62 (1993), 37–58.

Morton, Adam. *On Evil.* New York: Routledge, 2004.

Nongbri, Brent. *Before Religion: A History of a Modern Concept.* New Haven, CT: Yale University Press, 2013.

Nussbaum, Martha C. *Hiding from Humanity: Disgust, Shame, and the Law.* Princeton, NJ: Princeton University Press, 2004.

Oppenheimer, D. M. "The Secret Life of Fluency." *Trends in Cognitive Sciences* 12 (2008), 237–241.

Parkin, David, ed. *The Anthropology of Evil.* Oxford: Basil Blackwell, 1985.

Perry, Adele. *Aqueduct: Colonialism, Resources, and the Histories We Remember.* Winnipeg: ARP Books, 2016.

Ricoeur, Paul. *The Symbolism of Evil.* Translated by Emerson Buchanan. Boston, MA: Beacon Press, 1969.

Rochat, Philippe. *Others in Mind: Social Origins of Self-Consciousness.* Cambridge: Cambridge University Press, 2009.

Rosengren, Karl S., Carl N. Johnson, and Paul L. Harris, eds. *Imagining the Impossible: Magical, Scientific, and Religious Thinking in Children.* Cambridge, Cambridge University Press, 2000.

Rozin, P., J. Haidt, and C. R. McCauley. "Disgust." In *Handbook of Emotions*, 3rd edition, 757–776. Edited by M. Lewis, J. M. Haviland-Jones, and L. Feldman Barrett. New York: Guilford Press, 2008.

Ruel, Malcolm. *Belief, Ritual, and the Securing of Life: Reflexive Essays on a Bantu Religion.* New York: E. J. Brill, 1997.

Sack, Daniel. *Whitebread Protestants: Food and Religion in American Culture.* New York: Palgrave, 2000.

Saler, Benson, Charles A. Ziegler, and Charles B. Moore. *UFO Crash at Roswell: The Genesis of a Modern Myth.* Washington, DC: Smithsonian Books, 2010.

Segal, Robert A. *Myth: A Very Short Introduction*, 2nd edition. Oxford: Oxford University Press, 2015.

Sinclair, Niigaan. "What Reconciliation Feels Like to People 'Locked in the Bathroom' for a Century." CBC. March 19, 2018. Retrieved from www. cbc.ca/news/indigenous/opinion-reconciliation-beyond94-1.457 8359.

Singer, Dorothy G. and Jerome L. Singer. *The House of Make-Believe: Children's Play and the Developing Imagination.* Cambridge, MA: Harvard University Press, 1992.

Singleton, Andrew. "No Sympathy for the Devil: Narratives about Evil." *Journal of Contemporary Religion* 16, no. 2 (2001), 177–191.

Smith, Jonathan Z. *Drudgery Divine: On the Comparison of Early Christianities and the Religions of Late Antiquity.* Chicago, IL: University of Chicago Press, 1990.

Smith, Jonathan Z. *Imagining Religion: From Babylon to Jonestown.* Chicago, IL: University of Chicago Press, 1982.

Smith, Jonathan Z. *Map Is Not Territory: Studies in the History of Religion.* Chicago, IL: University of Chicago Press, 1993.

Smith, Jonathan Z. *Relating Religion: Essays in the Study of Religion*. Chicago, IL: University of Chicago Press, 2004.

Stoddard, Brad and Craig Martin, eds. *Stereotyping Religion: Critiquing Clichés*. New York: Bloomsbury Press, 2017.

Stoker, Bram. *Dracula*. New York: Penguin Classics, 2011.

Subbotsky, Eugene. *Magic and the Mind: Mechanisms, Functions, and Development of Magical Thinking and Behavior*. Oxford: Oxford University Press, 2010.

Taylor, Marjorie. *Imaginary Companions and the Children Who Create Them*. New York: Oxford University Press, 2001.

Taylor, Marjorie., ed. *The Oxford Handbook of the Development of Imagination*. New York: Oxford University Press, 2013.

Tomasello, Michael. *Cultural Origins of Human Cognition*. Cambridge, MA: Harvard University Press, 2009.

Tomasello, Michael. *Origins of Human Communication*. Cambridge, MA: MIT Press, 2010.

Trout, Paul A. "Shame on You." *CAUT Bulletin*. December 2006. Retrieved from https://bulletin-archives.caut.ca/bulletin/articles/2006/12/shame-on-you.

Truth and Reconciliation Commission of Canada. *Canada's Residential Schools: The History, Part 1. Origins to 1939*. Montreal: McGill-Queen's University Press, 2015. Retrieved from http://caid.ca/TRCFinVol1Par12015.pdf.

Truth and Reconciliation Commission of Canada. *Final Report of the Truth and Reconciliation Commission of Canada. Volume One: Summary. Honouring the Truth, Reconciling for the Future*. Toronto: Lorimer, 2015.

Walton, Kendall. *Mimesis as Make-Believe: On the Foundations of Representational Arts*. Cambridge, MA: Harvard University Press, 1993.

Warne, Randi R. "(En)gendering Religious Studies." *Studies in Religion/Sciences Religieuses* 27, no. 4 (1998), 427–436.

Watson, James L. "Funeral Specialists in Cantonese Society: Pollution, Performance, and Social Hierarchy." In *Death Ritual in Late Imperial and Modern China*, 109–134. Edited by James L. Watson and Evelyn S. Rawski. Berkeley, CA: University of California Press, 1990.

Watson, James L. and Rubie S. Watson. *Village Life in Hong Kong: Politics, Gender, and Ritual in the New Territories*. Hong Kong: Chinese University Press, 2004.

Wiebe, Donald. *The Irony of Theology and the Nature of Religious Thought*. Montréal: McGill-Queen's University Press, 1991.

Wiebe, Donald. *The Politics of Religious Studies: The Continuing Conflict with Theology in the Academy*. New York: Palgrave, 1999.

Wilson, Liz. *Charming Cadavers: Horrific Figurations of the Feminine in Indian Buddhist Hagiographic Literature.* Chicago, IL: University of Chicago Press, 1996.

Younging, Gregory. *Elements of Indigenous Style: A Guide for Writing By and About Indigenous Peoples.* Edmonton: Brush, 2018.

Index

Note: page numbers followed by *n* indicate notes.